MW01093708

Nothing to Lose

But Your Life

Nothing to Lose But Your Life

An 18-hour Journey with Murad

Suad Amiry

دار بلومزبري ـ مؤسسة قطر للنشر
BLOOMSBURY
QATAR FOUNDATION
PUBLISHING

مؤسسة قطر
Qatar Foundation

First published in 2010
Bloomsbury Qatar Foundation Publishing
Qatar Foundation
Villa 3, Education City
PO Box 5825
Doha, Qatar
www.bqfp.com.qa

ISBN 978-99921-42-05-9
99921-42-05-7

Cover by Nour Bishouty

Typeset by Hewer Text UK Ltd, Edinburgh

As I see it, it is wrong to write about people without living through at least a little of what they are living through.

Ryszard Kapuscinski,
Another Day of Life

Hence I accompanied Murad and his friends on a journey that lasted eighteen hours.

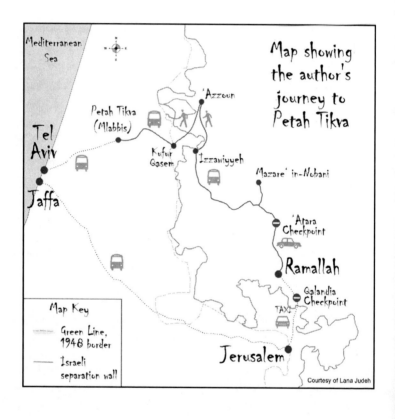

Map showing the author's journey to Petah Tikva

Mediterranean Sea

Tel Aviv

Jaffa

Petah Tikva (Mlabbis)

'Azzoun

Kufur Qasem

Izzawiyyeh

Mazare' in-Nobani

'Atara Checkpoint

Ramallah

Qalandia Checkpoint

TAXI

Jerusalem

Map Key

Green Line, 1948 border

Israeli separation wall

Courtesy of Lana Judeh

At first he seemed Palestinian
And when I looked intently at him he looked Mexican.
With the nightfall he looked African or perhaps
African-American,
Then Moroccan . . . then Algerian . . . then Turkish

Then I decided the dedication must be for all:

For Murad and Friends.

CONTENTS

1. Little Boys, Big Boys   1

2. Dummies Replacing Dummies   6

3. Only Once   17

4. Prisons are for Men   33

5. Good Morning, Palestine   40

6. One Thousand and One Arabian Nights   46

7. Night Hunters   61

8. Nothing to Lose But Your Life   73

9. Renewed Hope   84

10. Nothing Makes Sense, Why Should I?   99

11. Animal's Nightmare   108

12. Banksy's Wall: Time for Hope   116

13. On the Other Side   119

14. On Their Side   120

15. Lost Chapter   133

16. Lost Right of Return   149

Acknowledgments   159

1.

Little Boys, Big Boys

Saturday May 12, 2007 [10:10 PM]
Ramallah

I pressed my tits in an attempt to hide them, if not totally then at least to flatten them as much as possible so they would pass for a man's well-built chest muscles. Neither their size nor their texture really helped: they were way too big, way too wobbly and way too soft. For close to half an hour I'd been twisting my body left, right, and centre in front of the long mirror in our bedroom. Salim, my part-time husband, had been away for almost four months and wouldn't be back for another two.

It had certainly become difficult for me to look like a man or act like one, not only because of my wobbly chest, but also because of the increasingly undulating lines of my robust figure: wide hips, plump tummy, big derrière, stocky legs and a bent and slightly rickety middle-aged woman's posture.

I'd stopped looking closely at myself in the mirror, so I hadn't realised that I now looked more and more womanly. I don't know exactly what happened. For so long, my tall, thin, athletic body, as well as my then small breasts, short hair and unpierced ears had all made it easy, if not to pass for a boy, then to at least look like one. This is how, in the past, I had joined the neighbourhood boys playing all sorts of games in narrow Mango Street in Jabal Amman.

'You've done it again,' my mother would reprimand me. I would giggle. 'For God's sake Susu, sit down when you pee-pee, you don't have to spoil all your shoes and shorts.'

'I can pee while standing as well!'

'I know you can . . . I see the results . . . but girls are not designed to pee standing up.'

I would laugh again.

'Believe me, all of us . . . well, maybe not your father,' she corrected herself, 'wanted a brother for Ayman, but we got you instead: a beautiful and, more importantly, intelligent and clever little girl.' I would keep quiet so as to give Mama a bit of time to praise me even more. Dad often gave me compliments but my mother was a tougher case.

'You don't need to pee-pee standing up, or to look like a boy, in order to play in the streets with them.'

'But Mama, I'm the only girl. Fadwa's mama says it isn't right to play with boys in the streets.'

'Don't listen to her. She doesn't know any better . . . nothing wrong with that. The boys won't eat you.'

There was something exciting about peeing while standing up. It made me feel stronger, in control (though I had nothing to steer) and on top of the world. Peeing while standing also gave me the shivers. And it gave my mother lots of laundry to do. As a child I tried hard to look like a boy, but at the same time I would get extremely upset and saddened if someone mistook me for one. I would be so outraged and I would cry.

'If you hate it so much, why do it then?' my mother would scold, and I would run out of the door, through a garden full of animals, up the two dozen steep steps and out onto the street. There all the members of my brother's gang would be: Nabil, Haidar, Boulus, Butrus, Muones, Abdelkarim, Mouffaq, Ghaith . . . more and more boys, and me. We'd play football, then shift to hide-and-seek, then table football, then billiards, then marbles, then seven stones, then *hadar badar* (a children's game played with a few sticks and stones). I may not have been as strong, but I was lighter, thinner and certainly faster than all of them. This gave me an edge. 'Like a gazelle or a Saluki dog,' my father would often comment.

Once more, I examined myself in the mirror, but still I didn't think I would pass for a man. I changed my blouse for one of Salim's baggy shirts. I must look like one of them, one of the Big Boys: an indistinguishable member of the group, an indistinguishable member of the 'tribe', an indistinguishable member of the Night Hunters. Looking at myself in the mirror brought to mind my brother.

'Let's play *Wa Islamah*,' my brother Ayman suggested once. *Wa Islamah* ('Oh Islam') was a 1962 Egyptian film starring the famous actor, Rushdi Abaza. The film was about a lowly woman (played by Lubna Abdulaziz) from a harem who rises up to lead the Egyptians against the fourteenth-century invasion of Tartar hordes. What my brother and I remembered most from that film was how the herds of cattle and all the little boys and girls were branded with hot irons so that they wouldn't get lost or stolen. Once the war ended they were easily identified.

I screamed '*Wa Islamah*!' and ran as fast as I could out of the door, through a wide terrace with two fountains and the garden full of animals.

'No . . . no, wait, we need to heat the hot irons first,' my brother said.

3

'Okay . . .' I waited. From behind high and low garden walls various members of our animal farm leapt, flew and jumped. There was Mickey, our cute black dog who often ran after me and gave me that jealous 'play with me' bark, and Sasha, our neurotic little monkey. Every time she saw me or my brother Ayman play or run she would find yet another occasion, or excuse, to go wild, bouncing, swinging and hanging by her long legs and arms from one tree branch to another. Each jump or swing of Sasha's would frighten my mother's hundred white pigeons so that they would fly from the branches in all directions.

I watched Ayman light a candle, tie the slender key of his school bag with some thin rope, and heat it over the flame. Once it became red hot the game started.

'Now run for your life!' he yelled.

I ran along the long terrace into the small courtyard, and into the house again through a side door. Around and around, around and around the same circle, with the key being reheated in between, until I was breathless. Our two white and light beige Arabian deer, Reem and Sukkar, stood there watching me, their big round black eyes lined with kohl expressing total love and support, even those of blind Sukkar.

Just as Ayman was about to get me, I threw myself, face down, onto the living-room sofa. He was on top of me, screaming '*Wa Islamah!*' and pressing the hot key against the back of my arm. I could hear and smell the sizzling of my own skin. With a lifetime *Wa Islamah* mark on the back of my upper arm, I was sure I could venture into this world without any fear that one day I would be lost or unrecognised during or after the many wars of my life.

4

And here I was, half a century later, standing in front of the mirror: I wasn't intending to play with the little boys of the neighbourhood.

Tonight, I was to play with Palestine's 'Big Boys'.

2.

Dummies Replacing Dummies

Saturday May 12, 2007 [10:25 PM]

From Ramallah to Mazare' in-Nobani

I've been a coward since childhood. Realising this, my mother would often recite this proverb: a thousand times a coward and not once a dead man. Lately, in the past week or so, I'd found myself repeating this proverb a thousand times: *Alf marrah jaban wala marrah allah yirhamo.*

I'd been anxious, worried and uncertain for two consecutive Saturdays and now, finally, it was ten twenty-five on Saturday night. I picked up the phone and called Murad's brother Mohammad.

'Let's go.' I kept it short and simple so as not to change my mind or reveal my high state of anxiety.

'Right away.' Mohammad's to-the-point reply only increased my anxiety. I hung up and ran to the toilet. I had the runs. In less than half an hour Mohammad arrived at our house.

'Let's go,' he said assertively, and we stepped out to the front door. His mobile phone rang. My heart skipped the first beat of many to come. For a while Mohammad kept quiet, listening intently. Finally, after a long pause, came his agitated reply: '*Khalas ya zalameh* . . . that's enough, man . . . no need to discourage us . . . we need a word of encouragement, not the opposite . . .' There seemed to be another round of protest.

6

'Here she is, you talk to her.' Mohammad handed me his mobile.

'My brother Maher wants to talk to you, Suad.'

'*Marhaba doctora Suad, keefek?* How are you?' Maher's high-pitched voice was deafening. I held the mobile the length of my long arm away from my ear and I could still hear his yells. He was shouting as if speaking from another planet. In reality, he was. I don't know what it is with us Palestinians; whenever we talk on the phone, especially long distance, we tend to shout at the top of our voices. Since the First World War, when the Ottomans introduced the phone to Palestine, we seem to have remained faithful to two of the Ottoman Empire's traditions: loud phone conversations and endless wars.

'Good evening, Maher,' I replied in a low voice, as normal as possible under the circumstances.

'Please, please doctora, don't come. It's going to be tough. It's not fitting for someone like you. Please don't listen to Mohammad; he's irresponsible and reckless and doesn't know what he's talking about. He hasn't been there for over ten years now. Things have changed, especially in the past year, even in the past few months. It gets worse by the day . . . by the hour . . .'

'Okay . . . okay . . . okay . . . okay, Maher . . . cool it . . . It's me who wants to come, not Mohammad . . . Don't you worry . . . we'll give it a try . . . If we succeed, fine; if not, we go back . . . Okay, Maher . . . see you soon.'

There was silence, then I heard Maher say, 'Okay, okay. *Inshallah* . . . with God's will . . . Let's hope so . . . Just be careful, don't take any risks.' Maher was resigned. I hung up and handed the phone back to Mohammad.

7

There was silence, and then more silence for some time to come.

Mohammad and I hid our growing anxiety by keeping quiet. The emptiness and darkness of the narrow and winding road didn't help.

'Did you bring your ID?' asked Mohammad, a welcome break in the dreadful silence.

'I brought my ID and some money,' I replied, sticking my hand into my pockets, but I had difficulty finding them while driving. I carefully stopped the car on the side of the road, stepped out, and searched my jacket and trousers. Finally I found my ID in the back pocket of my trousers. I felt my money in the front one. Yes, now I remembered: I had made sure to separate them so that my money would be safe when I showed my ID to the soldiers at the checkpoint. I got back in the car and drove along the dark road once more.

There was hardly anybody on the road between Ramallah and Birzeit. And there was hardly any other road in Palestine that I knew better, as it happened to be the road I'd taken to work at Birzeit University for more than fifteen years. It also happened to be one of the very few roads that the Israeli army hadn't obstructed, as they did with all the other tiny run-down Palestinian roads, as opposed to the Israeli settlers' newly constructed highways.

It was past eleven at night when I took my ID out of my pocket in preparation for the Israeli soldiers at 'Atara check-point, one of the three hundred and sixty checkpoints sepa-rating Palestine from Palestine. This particular one separated

Ramallah from other Palestinian towns and villages located in the northern district of Nablus.

Mohammad did the same. He got his ID out of his pocket and prepared himself psychologically to be checked. He combed back his long black hair with his fingers.

'We're going to visit your family . . . right?' I wanted to make sure that Mohammad and I gave exactly the same responses to the Israeli soldiers when asked where we were heading at this late hour.

'Right,' was Mohammad's brief reply.

Once more, Mohammad and I were quiet, this time in anticipation of our first checkpoint encounter.

I made sure to slow down as we approached the checkpoint. I was carefully looking out for one of the five or six soldiers to wave his hand and indicate that we should slowly (and cautiously) come closer. I would switch off the ignition of the car in order to have our IDs checked and our car searched. But I couldn't see anyone.

'Do you see any soldiers?' I asked Mohammad.

'No, I don't.'

'Look carefully . . . we don't want any incidents this early on.'

'I swear to God, I see no one.'

'No need to swear, just look carefully. Look inside the watchtower on your right.'

'How can I tell? Sometimes the soldiers put dummies inside the watchtowers and then leave.'

'Dummies replacing dummies,' I angrily replied.

Mohammad laughed. He stretched his head out first, then the upper half of his body, from the car window, looking carefully up at the high round concrete tower hovering above us.

'I see no dummies, do you?'

'Can't see the tower from my side, Mohammad.' I was getting agitated.

'Then . . . what shall we do?' He sounded confused.

'Shall I carry on?' I asked.

'I guess so, but slowly and carefully.'

I opened all the windows so we could hear them if they should suddenly appear and yell at us. For the first kilometre I was driving at one . . . metre . . . per . . . hour.

Still there was nobody. I carefully and anxiously proceeded, anticipating the first shot in the air, another through the back window, a third in the head, but none arrived. I must say, it would have been less nerve-wracking handling the presence of the Israeli soldiers than their absence. We'd become so used to their forty-odd-year 'presence' that a one-night absence seemed absolutely unbearable.

With a carefully calculated acceleration we proceeded. At first we were guided by the bright lights of the wide road used by the Israeli settlers, but soon after, we moved through the darkness of the narrow road, undulating down and up through the olive tree-studded valleys, taking us to Murad's village, Mazare' in-Nobani.

I wondered what contributed more to the deserted and eerie feel of our roads: the Palestinian provincial lifestyle (no style), sleeping early and not venturing out at night, or the Israeli occupation? Or perhaps people stopped venturing out at night because of the occupation? It was a catch-22 situation. Whether we're the chicken or the egg, we're certainly contributing to making their/our occupation a part-time responsibility. And that perhaps explained why the cosmopolitan Palestinian PLO returnees, who lived in Beirut and Tunis, couldn't take either the Israeli occupation or Palestinian provinciality. Since it was a daytime occupation, it wasn't surprising that there were no Israeli soldiers at Surda's checkpoint. Looking on the brighter side of things, by sleeping so much we had managed to become totally resilient to their brutal occupation. I couldn't begin to imagine what the Milanese, Neapolitans, Parisians or Londoners would do if put under curfew for thirty or forty consecutive days.

I could theorise no more, as Mohammad was clearly determined to keep me company all the way. He told me about every nerve-wracking encounter he, his eight brothers, his father, his uncles, his numerous friends, and even 'someone' he knew, had ever had with the Israeli army. As he frequently moved between his work place in Ramallah and this village, Mazare' in-Nobani, Mohammad had many such stories related to this spooky road.

'Last year, during the month of Ramadan, I was fasting and wanted to get home before sunset. I was eager to be with members of my family for my mother's *ftur* (the sunset meal ending the day-long fast during Ramadan). There were hundreds of cars lined up in both directions at a flying checkpoint at the Israeli settlement of Dolev. So the four of us decided to turn back and take this road, the road we're on tonight . . . Oh God, what a terrible mistake it was . . . we were almost killed. In no time all, at all hell broke loose . . . Before we knew it, we were surrounded by four soldiers, one for each of the four of us, with rifles at point blank at our four heads . . . "Out!" they screamed . . . and we got out of the Beetle. One poor old man was shaking as he begged the

11

soldiers not to push him. Our car was searched inside out, we were searched, and stripped almost naked, and finally we were kept hostage inside Dolev for hours and hours . . . "Now you can go and have *suhur* (the meal eaten before sunrise in Ramadan) with your families," the soldiers said, laughing as they let us go. It was almost two o'clock in the morning.'

'And what time is it now?' I interrupted Mohammad's never-ending stream of high-adrenaline stories. His accounts reminded me of a flight I'd once taken over the Atlantic. In order to relax and pass the time during that flight, we were shown a film about an impending plane crash and its hysterical passengers. That film lasted for only part of the flight, but Mohammad's accounts continued throughout the whole trip.

While Mohammad fumbled around in search of his mobile to check the time, I looked at the dashboard and saw that it wasn't yet midnight. I also noticed that there was hardly any petrol left. Not venturing out of Ramallah's checkpoints for months now, and hardly using third gear while driving short distances, I had lost the habit of checking the petrol before travelling. It was in the red.

'Eleven-forty,' he replied.

'Guess what, Mohammad? We're running out of petrol.'

'Don't worry, there's a petrol station right here.'

I looked sideways. Mohammad was right. There was something that resembled a petrol station. Like the 'Atara checkpoint, it was deserted.

'Don't worry, we're almost home.' One less thing to worry about.

Before I even had the chance to worry about being stuck in the middle of the eerie valley, Mohammad started another horror story, 'Once, I was . . .'

12

This torrent of nightmarish stories was very unlike Mohammad, I must say. The tension must've been welling up inside him. In reality, one of Mohammad's most endearing qualities was his discretion. His baby face, the look of serenity, the droopy brown eyes and small white teeth all contributed to his pleasant and naïve looks. It only took a single word from Mohammad, followed by a mischievous smile, for me and my colleagues to realise that he understood everything.

He particularly understood the complexity and intricacy of personal dynamics between the fifteen characters working at Riwaq*. In the twelve years he'd been there, he had managed to make close and personal friends with every single one of us. Being the office boy, or to put it in a more politically correct way, the administrative assistant, Mohammad had manoeuvrability, not only in and out of Riwaq, but also between our offices.

Mohammad demonstrated his clout in the office through the selection of what we all ate in our daily communal brunch. From the choices he made and the quality of the brunch we could tell his mood and who among us was his favourite that particular day. Through his three to four daily rounds of excellent Turkish coffee, with lots of cardamom, Mohammad managed to gather a wealth of information, and this certainly gave him an edge that he never seemed to abuse.

On weekends, Mohammad often went to see his family, particularly his mother Safiyyeh whom he simply adored. He often bragged about her food, especially his favourite dish *maqloubeh*, which literally means 'upside down' because of the way the pan is flipped onto a huge dish before being served.

* Riwaq is a cultural heritage NGO based in Ramallah.

13

'No one, no one, makes *maqloubeh* the way my mother does.' I'd heard this one before.

'She never uses Uncle Ben's, only the tasty Egyptian rice.' A good start, I thought.

'As for the type of aubergine, when it's in season, she only uses Batiri.'* An overstatement, but never mind.

'She soaks them in salty water, so as not to absorb too much oil, and then fries them until they become golden.' Common sense, to us women.

'Once they're fried, she puts them on layers and layers of paper towels so as not to make the *maqloubeh* too greasy.' Another obvious remark.

'She cuts and boils lots of carrots and potatoes on the side. As for the meat, of course it has to be *kharouf* and not *eijel* (lamb and not veal).' Lamb . . . a bit stinky, I'd vote no. With so many unnecessary and mundane details, my head was turning upside down, but still, his recipes were better than his army horror stories. Mohammad took a breath, as did I, but he carried on.

'Once the meat is cooked, with lots of spices, cardamom, cumin and nutmeg, she places it in a circle at the bottom of a huge pan.' I tried to imagine the size of the pan that could feed at least fifteen members of Mohammad's family.

'Then she places the carrots and potatoes on top, and then she carefully lays the slices of fried aubergine in yet another layer. At the end, she drops the rice in the pan and covers it all in a meat broth. She leaves it to cook for thirty or forty minutes on a very, very, very low heat. When it's done, she

---

* Batir is the name of a village south of Bethlehem, famous for its small tasty purple aubergines.

wraps the pan in a special woolen blanket and leaves it to settle for ten minutes.'

'And?' I enquired.

'And with the help of one of my brothers, she flips it upside down and lays it in the middle of the floor, like a colourful wedding cake, around which the whole family gathers. She makes two kinds of side salad: one is yogurt with garlic and the other is tomatoes with cumin and *ya 'ein, ya 'ein*, mmm, yummy yummy!' Oh how I wished it wasn't all talk.

It was no longer clear to me whom or what he adored more, his mother Safiyyeh or her cooking. But isn't food the sauce of every man's Oedipus complex?

Soon, we were in the centre of Mazare' in-Nobani. There was hardly anyone in its dark and winding streets. The few lights coming out of the small old stone houses and the new concrete boxes indicated that some were already having sweet dreams (or nightmares), while others were more likely watching television. We soon passed by the deserted historic village centre where there was not a single light.

All was dark, quiet and serene except for a reverberation that sounded intermittently. We drove through the non-descript new 'village centre' past an even more non-descript tiny coffee shop where a dozen or more young men were watching TV. From their cheering I gathered they were watching a football match.

Mohammad asked me to stop the car. I did so, and in no time at all, Mazen, yet another brother, greeted us and promised to join us at home once the match was over, his eyes remaining fixated on the television screen the whole time.

15

I was anxious to be with Murad and his family.

'Why so late in the coffee shop?'

'There is nothing for him to do except pass the time in Ibrahim's coffee shop,' said Mohammad. My first impulse was to ask, 'But how will they get up for work tomorrow morning?' I stopped myself just in time.

I was eager to know what was awaiting me that night. I parked my car on the steep, almost vertical, dirt road right in front of Mohammad's family's new two-storey concrete house. I could smell the still burning *taboun* oven. The combined aroma of smoke, manure, and freshly baked bread made me realise how hungry I was.

The minute we stepped into the darkness of their garden, the donkey 'barked' while the dog simply wagged its tail. In the distance, opposite, I could see a flood of strong orange lights marking the middle of a wide road. The newly constructed Israeli settlements occupied the very top of that same hill. It was almost midnight when Mohammad and I stepped into a room dimly lit by a quivering television light.

3.

Only Once

It took a while for my eyes to adjust to the semi-darkness of the room. And it took a bit longer to figure out who was who, and who was where, in a living-sleeping room with mattresses spread along the length of two walls.

As soon as we entered, I spotted Abu Maher.* He was lying on the bare floor next to the television. The faint colours of the old set made me recall the late fifties in my grandfather's house in the old town of Damascus, where a three-colour (blue, pink and green) plastic sheet was placed over the black and white television screen. The dimness and ambience of that room somehow triggered a deep nostalgia for my grandfather's 'television room'.

I vividly recalled the excitement of all the members of our extended family as we stood in the huge courtyard with the fountain in the middle. My aunts and uncles half-stood, half-sat, half-bent over the black and white marble edge of the fountain, while we children spun around and around, in and out, out and in, checking on my grandfather. We were anxiously waiting for him to appear with the black and white

---

* Meaning, the Father of Maher. In Arabic, fathers are often referred to as the father of the eldest son. The mother is referred to as Umm Maher.

17

television set he had ordered six months earlier through the central government. None of us children had the faintest idea what a television set looked like. 'It's a home cinema,' the older people said.

After an hour or so, my tall and rather handsome grandfather stepped into the courtyard. With his white turban wrapped around his head, he proudly walked a step or two in front of two porters with Popeye muscles. One giant was crouched under the weight of the wooden box. He had wrapped a wide band around his head, his body and the TV. I vividly remember how I, my brother Ayman, my two sisters and the tens of cousins and neighbourhood kids followed the porters into a room which my aunts had emptied the day before of all other furniture except for the two divans that ran along two walls, similar to Abu Maher's mattresses.

For years to come there was a strong belief that 'television rooms' like movie houses, must be completely dark during the four television transmission hours of six to ten in the evening. It often took a while for my eyes to adjust before I could make out my favourite cousin, Mohannad. Once that happened, I would squeeze my lean body next to his, hoping that none of the many TV viewers, especially my aunt, Suad, whom we all feared, would notice my very first and everlasting crush on him.

Abu Maher's skinny body was lost in the shabby trousers and half-open shirt that showed his late-sixty-ish wrinkled, dark olive-coloured skin. His small head somehow looked 'comfortable' resting on the sharp angle of the concrete. His long moustache, his tiny sharp features and his small, black and piercing fox-like eyes were accentuated by the light coming from the television.

To release some of the mounting unease at disturbing them at this odd hour of the night, I rushed to greet him with a high-pitched-voice (not as high as Maher's, but still . . .) and over-the-top enthusiasm.

'*Masa al-khair,* Abu Maher, how are you?'

He sat up and shook my hand. 'Good evening, doctora,' he said, which sounded more like, 'Good evening, you *crazy* thing.'

Abu Maher, like his son in the coffee shop, was obviously mesmerised by the television, and rarely spoke in the few hours I spent in the same room with him. Unlike Mazen, who was having a great time screaming at the football players, Abu Maher was despondent in front of the TV. My heart sank as I glanced quickly at the screen in order to figure out if his captivity was caused by yet another Israeli strike on Gaza, or, even worse, a total closure of the West Bank, making our mission tonight even more difficult. But no: Abu Maher was not at all burdened by trivial local news. He was watching the widely admired television series, *Andalusia: The Lost Heaven.*

'It is unfair and completely unethical,' complained my next-door neighbour in Ramallah once, when his car was stolen while he sat watching *The Lost Heaven.* 'Of course the whole town is immersed in this programme, the streets are completely empty, and no one could spot thieves during this hour.' Being one of the very few who did not watch this or any other television series, I could attest to the fact that Ramallah felt as if it was under curfew whenever either this or the Egyptian espionage episodes of *Raafat Al-Haggan** were on

★ Raafat Al-Haggan was an Egyptian spy whose life was the subject of a famous television series.

television. I soon realised, that like the rest of the Palestinians, and 250 million other Arabs, Abu Maher was mourning the loss of Andalusia in 1492, which was the subject of the Syrian television series.

Having a Syrian mother myself, I recognised the phenomenon of dwelling on the glory of the past rather than dealing with the harsh realities of today (meaning my father).

'Why don't you switch the light on?' I heard Umm Maher say as she appeared from an adjacent room, wrapping her short red hennaed hair in a small green scarf. She wore a dark green velvet dress, rather than a nightgown, which clung tightly to her pointed tummy and her high, protruding and rounded buttocks. While her husband had rather handsome features, Umm Maher was not particularly pretty, but she had a kind expression with soft features: small brown eyes, a rounded nose, full lips and high blushing apple-like cheeks. And unlike Abu Maher, Umm Maher had a rather simple and straightforward character.

Umm Maher was followed by her teenage daughter, whose name, like some of her nine brothers, I didn't know then and still don't know now. Unlike her brothers, she had a light complexion and wavy blondish hair. The soft, gentle look on her face reminded me of Mohammad. The sky-blue tracksuit that she wore matched her delightful green eyes nicely.

'Sorry . . . sorry, really sorry for waking you up, Umm Maher . . . Go back to sleep . . . Please go back to sleep,' I insisted.

'Not at all, not at all, *ahla o sahla* doctora . . . You're most welcome . . . Welcome, most welcome . . . Sit down . . . A thousand welcomes . . . Sit here, sit down here . . . Bring the doctora some cushions, bring her more cushions . . . Go make the doctora tea . . . or is it coffee you prefer, doctora? *Ya mieet ahlan wa sahlan*, a hundred welcomes.'

As she devotedly welcomed me, she gave orders to her son, Mohammad, and to her daughter. They were both running around the house trying to make the doctora comfortable by piling more and more, and even more, cushions around me.

'Here, take this,' said Mohammad as he handed me two big colourfully embroidered cushions.

'Thanks, Mohammad.' Before I had had a chance to admire the beautiful silken cushions and to enquire who had spent so much time embroidering them, Mohammad's sister handed me three more navy blue velvet cushions.

'Thank you, dear, thank you, *habibti*, really, thanks. No need for more, enough, really enough.' While I slipped the blue velvet cushions behind my back, Umm Maher joined the cushion frenzy, disappearing into her own room and returning hurriedly in my direction.

'Get up . . . get up doctora . . . Move your back a bit this way . . . no, no, that way, put these behind your back, and the velvet ones on the side.' She handed me two huge heavy square pillows in rough fabric. The striking purple and blue floral design made me feel as if I was sitting in the midst of Versailles Gardens, a photo studio in Ramallah.

'Thanks, thanks,' I repeated as I tried to figure out how to float on an ocean of pillows. Mohammad handed me three more. Finally I was saved from drowning in a colourful sea of cushions by the phone ringing in the adjacent room: ring, ring, ring, ring . . . ring, ring, ring. Umm Maher ran to get it. From a distance I heard her shouting 'Allo . . . allooo . . . allo . . . Who's speaking? Allo . . . Who is it you want? It was you who called, not me. I know, but who is speaking? What

21

number did you call? What number did you want? Oh, did you want Mazen? Yes, *this is* Umm Maher. Oh, hello Ahmad, how are you? I'll have him call you back. Bye . . . bye . . . bye . . . bye . . . Okay . . . bye.'

You may think I am exaggerating but believe me there is no other culture, language, or people who repeat as much as we do. Do you know of any other language that has expressions to express abundance such as these? *Hakena haki*: we talked such talks; *shribna shurub*: we drank such drinks; *akalna akl*: we ate such eats. We played such plays. We laughed such laughs. We ran such runs. And so ridiculously repetitious it goes.

Back to Umm Maher: I was so cushioned I could hardly reach the tea tray that was soon placed on the floor right in front of me. I couldn't help but think again of the way Abu Maher's head was resting on that concrete angle. But realising that these cushions, and many other objects and delicacies besides, were meant for, and appeared only for the guests, I didn't violate the rules of hospitality by offering Abu Maher one of my cushions.

Now that I was all settled the real conversation started.

'*Keefek doctora? Inshallah meneeha*? How are you doctora? Hope you're well? *Keef doctor Salim? Inshallah mneeh*? How is Dr. Salim? Hope he is well? How is your sister? *Inshallah mneehea?* Hope she is well, hopefully better? And how is Umm Salim? Oh, so sorry . . . May her soul rest in peace.'

'Fine, thanks . . . fine, thanks . . . fine . . . Yes, may God bless her soul, yes, she passed away last year.'

I was so taken by Umm Maher's overwhelming hospitality that it took me a while to realise that the person stretched out on the mattress right opposite me was Murad.

'*Habibi* darling, Murad, get up . . . *al-doctora* Suad has arrived. Get up and greet her.'

Half-asleep, and with his eyes half-closed, Murad got up from his mattress. Yawning, he held out his hand to greet me. I tried to stand up but the tens of cushions around me made it impossible. As both our arms stretched across the room, Murad effortlessly bounced up and down, making it possible for us finally to shake hands.

I had totally forgotten how tiny Murad was. His navy blue boxers and white string vest revealed skinny legs with protruding knees, thin but muscular arms and rather narrow, but straight shoulders. Though I'd known Murad for a number of years, I seemed to recall a stronger and fiercer body; it must have been the many gang stories he had told me in the past that had left me with the impression that he was physically much bigger. I re-examined him, but this time I was reassured by the many fight scars he had on his hands, his neck and the parts of his head which were not covered by his spiky hairstyle. I felt more confident remembering how well-built and tough he was in spite of his small size. The inquisitive expression in Murad's shining, hazelnut eyes, framed by his thick black eyebrows and the pale smile on his sleepy face, encouraged me to ask,

'Do you still want to take us with you tonight?' I smiled.

'Only if you want,' Murad said in his usual blasé style.

'After a few weeks of hesitation, here I am.' I replied.

'But doctora, why do you want to do this?' asked Umm Maher inquisitively. Before I had time to gather my thoughts she carried on, 'No, truly, doctora, why put yourself through this? You don't know how many times Maher has called this evening. He's been begging me to convince you not to go, doctora,' insisted Umm Maher.

23

'We know . . . we know, Mother, he also called me and talked to doctora Suad.' I was glad Mohammad answered on my behalf.

'You may get shot at . . .' said Abu Maher casually, taking a one-second break from his Andalusian soap opera.

'WHAT . . . SHOT AT? You don't really mean it, do you?' I asked frantically, even though I'd known that all along. But somehow I didn't like it when it got personal, which was exactly why I had hesitated to make this trip for such a long time.

'No . . . don't listen to him, what does he know? In the eight years I've been going, it's only lately they've started shooting at us. And *only once* did they shoot dead a worker, and *only once* did they shoot someone in the leg. He fell right next to me,' said Murad, again in his nonchalant way.

That *only once* really got to me. Soon I was talking to myself:

Oh my God . . . Suad, are you sure you want to do this?

All it takes is to be shot at *only once*.

Only once and you'll be dead and never have a chance to write this *bloody* book . . .

Only a pretentious bourgeois, a romantic and a leftist like me would think she could represent the underdog: workers, women and children. Not to speak of the animal kingdom. And here I was trying to collect material for my new book by being adventurous *only once,* then playing around with the material (people's lives) and writing a brilliant book about the remaining 150,000 Palestinian workers who were feeding a million.

In the year 2000, when the second uprising erupted, Sharon cancelled all work permits, and so overnight over 150,000 workers lost their jobs in Israel after having worked there for more than thirty-three years (from 1967 to 2000). And with a complete economic dependency on Israel, the disjointed and disconnected Occupied Territories hadn't much to offer.

And here I am, in total sympathy, in the middle of the night, waking up not only the poor worker Murad, but his mother, his sister, his brother, his other brother, the whole family, so as to accommodate my own writing.

'Come on, they shoot at you all the time,' said Abu Maher, half-asleep, his head still resting on the concrete sharp angle.

'Yes, but mostly in the air.'

'Drink your tea, doctora,' said the mother.

I picked up my tea and gulped it down in one go. It felt like a shot of Russian vodka.

Only when I got tipsy did I realise that there was one more person under the pink sheet on the mattress to my right. 'Who is it?' I asked, in an attempt to distract myself.

'It's Fadi,' answered Umm Maher. She stretched from her mattress and tickled him. I could hear Fadi giggling, and his small body shifted under the pink sheet.

'How old is he?' I enquired.

'Thirteen.'

'I was his age when I started working in Israel,' said Murad.

'And how old are you now?'

'Twenty-one.'

'Twenty-one! Still a baby,' I said.

'I worked for over thirty-seven years in Israel,' shouted Abu Maher.

'I worked for four years: eleven to fifteen, until I came to work on the construction site with you, doctora. Was it '95 or '96?' Mohammad asked me.

'Maybe even earlier. Of course I remember it as if it were yesterday when Maher brought you and Mazen to work on that construction site. You were a young boy then. I felt bad allowing you on the site; that's why you ended up in the office at Riwaq.'

'I wish you could help Murad find work in Ramallah, doctora,' said the mother shyly.

'I hate working with Arabs. Who told you I wanted to work in Ramallah?' Murad lit a cigarette and pulled up one side of his shorts as he sat cross-legged on the edge of his mattress.

'*Yamma,** Murad, look at you my son . . . you've got to get started at two-thirty in the morning, sleep in the wilderness like a fugitive, with no toilets, no baths, not a single hot meal. Is that a life, son? I worry about you . . . Believe me, doctora, there's not a single hour of peaceful sleep for me while he, Maher and Majed are away.'

'Give me another option and I'll take it . . . *bidna n'eesh, Yamma.* We want to live, Mother,' emphasised Murad.

'Work in Ramallah,' she argued.

'Find me a job in Ramallah or anywhere else in the West Bank and I'll take it.'

'No, you won't.'

'No, I won't.'

'Hell . . . what do Arabs pay, fifty shekels a day, seventy max? When you can earn a hundred and fifty in Israel?'

'That's if you find work.'

'I always do.'

---

* Although *yamma* is literally an address to a 'mother', in Palestine mothers often use it to address their children.

26

'For a day or two, then what?'

'Sometimes for a whole week.'

Not wanting to depress her beloved son, Umm Maher changed her tone. *'Allah yaateek al-afiyyeh o yes'edak, yamma.* May God keep you healthy and happy, son.'

'Would you like to eat something, doctora?'

'No thanks, Umm Maher, I'm not hungry.'

'Go prepare dinner for the doctora.'

The young sister stood up and disappeared.

'No . . . no really, thanks. I'm not hungry, really.'

'You soon will be,' she said, adding, 'You need to eat and get some sleep. What time is the Ford coming to pick you up, Murad?'

'Two-thirty.' I looked at my watch; it was already well past midnight.

Murad offered me a cigarette while we waited for dinner.

'No . . . no thanks. I quit smoking almost a year ago. A dear friend of mine died of lung cancer last July and since then I swore not to touch another cigarette, and I haven't since.'

'You see . . . she stopped after so many years of smoking. Son, why don't you do the same?' Umm Maher addressed her Murad in an overly protective motherly way.

'If he quits smoking then perhaps the fifty or seventy "Arab shekels" would be enough. He spends most of the money he makes in Israel, either on cigarettes or on that Russian slut,' said Abu Maher. Hysterical laughter rose from everyone in the room, including Murad.

'What Russian slut?' I asked, amused.

'She's not Russian, she's Moroccan.'

'Worse,' said the father, while the smoke of his own cigarette made nearby Granada pretty foggy.

'She's not Moroccan, she's Yemeni.'

'Even worse.'

'Who is she?' I leaned over and whispered not so discreetly to Mohammad.

'His lover,' Mohammad replied loudly.

'And . . . ?'

'My father thinks she's a prostitute.'

'Is she?'

'NO . . . but I don't think she's in love with Murad . . . She teases him.'

'Like a fool, he spends his money on her while she's in love with Saed.'

'Who's Saed?' I asked, as the plot thickened around me.

'Murad's best friend. You'll meet him tonight.'

'Wow . . . Juicy stuff.'

'Ya . . . sure, I spend my money on her! She's the one who spends her money on me.'

'*Wala bil ahlam* . . . *ya* . . . *ya* . . . not in your wildest dreams, son,' replied Abu Maher from his comfortable position on the cement floor.

The give and take between Abu Maher and Murad sounded more like an argument between peers. As the two argued, Mazen, Mohammad's younger brother, stepped into the room. With his usual sweet smile and his big droopy eyes and friendly and delicate face he came to greet me,

'*Offffff* . . . Not again . . . Russian . . . Moroccan . . . Yemeni. Anyway, why bother when she's in love with Saed!' said Mazen as he burst into loud laughter, slapping his palms together.

Mazen shook my hand and disappeared into the adjacent room. Soon after, he came back with a small photo album. He walked slowly towards me and handed me the photo album with a twinkle in his eye.

What joy!

There was Murad with his girl; her blonde, Russian-looking hair contrasting sharply with her bronze Moroccan or Yemeni complexion. There they were in front of a high-rise building, in a restaurant, on the seashore, on one chair with her hand stretched across his lap, his arm on the chair behind her.

'Is this in Tel Aviv?' was my first wary enquiry.

'No, in Petah Tikva.'

'So I get a chance to see her tomorrow?' I asked jokingly. 'Is this her mother?'

'No, this is her employer, the owner of the restaurant. She is such a good woman, she feeds us, jokes with us, and when we're in need, she lends us money.'

'Oh Rifqa, both she and the *Yahoodi* (Jew, meaning an Israeli) owner of the garage are really kind to us,' said Mazen in his agreeable tone while slouching on the only sofa in the room.

The photo album gave me a golden opportunity to end my suffering, sitting cross-legged all this time. Both my ankles, my knees and both hips cracked one after the other, making a non-athletic middle-aged urban tune as I stood up, straightened my legs and went to sit on the sofa next to Mazen. So much for acting modestly and sitting cross-legged on the floor. Sitting comfortably on the sofa, I flipped back and forth through Murad and Lily's love story. Soon I was mesmerised by the many other facets of Murad's character(s) and life(s).

There was Murad the worker: one photo showed him posing next to a counter of what seemed to be a small sandwich outlet; the orange sign with a red frame had an image of a baguette next to a chilled glass of lemonade with a slice of lemon on the edge. The spotlessly clean black counter against which Murad leaned, as well as the shining silver cooker and the two emptied garbage containers behind him all suggested that he was enjoying his end-of-the-day cigarette.

Another Murad end-of-work photo showed him sitting on an iron bed with a red mattress with no sheets. The bed was placed in the open, probably in a factory yard. The sign behind him read 'Emergency exit to the lobby', but the lobby to what I could not tell. Murad sat in the middle of the bed. To his right was a wrinkled blue and bright yellow cover and to his left a matching blue pillow. Murad looked truly tired; he had dark circles under his eyes; he was unshaven and sweaty. The thick gauze bandage around his palm indicated that he must have seriously hurt himself.

'What happened to your hand?' I asked, moving from Murad's album to the real Murad.

'That stupid old Yahoodi employer wouldn't move his bloody dog. I went to work for him. He wanted me to knock down a concrete room in his garden. He had a huge dog right next to me that kept barking whenever I moved, and when I asked him to take his bloody dog away he refused. I was so angry at him I cursed him and threw a big stone at his dog. He was so outraged that he ran after me and threatened to report me to the police. I pushed him and ran away but I fell over and ripped my palm open on a broken beer bottle.'

All of a sudden I remembered the day that Murad first came to help me in the garden of my house in Ramallah.

30

That day, Murad told me this and many other heartbreaking stories. That was the day I decided to accompany him.

Back to the photo album.

There was Murad the playboy stretching half-naked on a bed next to a wall with nine medium-sized posters of women models in bikinis. It seemed that Murad had torn these out of a swimsuit catalogue. The expression on his face, particularly his half-closed eyes, indicated that he had probably asked whoever was taking his photograph to be left alone for a while.

There was also Murad the fun and nature lover, posing in different parks under different trees, or on the beach. One photograph in particular caught my eye; it must have been his ridiculous-looking sunglasses (dark and oval-shaped with a thin silver rim) and his even more ridiculous hairstyle, all shaven around the head except the middle part which fell to the front like an Elvis Presley quiff. Murad had a dove of peace necklace around his neck and a bracelet on his wrist in this photograph. With a big bottle of Amstel beer between his bare feet, he sat on one of many rocks, a rough sea behind him.

There was also Murad the fighter, or, more accurately, Murad the hunter: with a Castro-like khaki uniform, hiding behind a low parapet while pointing his rusted First World War rifle towards his target. Examining the details of the surroundings, I could tell this photo was taken in the garden of this house. Caught with this or any other rifle in Israel, Murad would be sentenced to at least three life sentences and this he knew very well.

And there was Murad the pious, as a little boy in front of the Dome of the Rock in Jerusalem. Or standing in a recent studio–posed photo with an incredibly serious face, his body slightly tilted, his arm bent and his finger pointing towards heaven. The background was a Swiss-like landscape: a path of huge flowering trees, also signifying heaven. The Arabic writing on his arm said *al-nasr qareeb* ('victory is near') while Murad's white ivory necklace matched nicely the white Hebrew writing on his black sleeveless T-shirt.

And finally there was Murad the musician: again in a posed studio photo, holding a Spanish guitar with a pink poster of a rough sea behind him. He looked happiest in this photo.

'Do you play the guitar?' I asked Murad, breaking the silence in the room.

He smiled and tilted his head upwards, indicating a 'no' gesture.

'Once it was a dream of mine,' he added.

4.

Prisons are for Men

Sunday May 13, 2007 [12:20 AM]
Still At Home

'I wish I could come with you,' said Mazen, deeply inhaling his cigarette. A few seconds later he playfully and slowly puffed out the smoke into the stuffy room.

'Why don't you come then?' I was a bit baffled.

'Can't.'

'Why not?'

'Didn't Mohammad tell you? He was arrested and imprisoned for a whole month,' Umm Maher answered on Mazen's behalf. She, like him, looked a bit sad.

'I was on my way to get my money from my Yahoodi employer, for work I'd done the week before, when the army arrested me. When I argued with the soldiers they beat me up and threw me in their jeep and took me straight to prison.'

I took a deep breath. My eyes followed Mazen's swirling smoke circles. 'Was it really bad? I mean, in the prison?'

'At first I was sad and depressed, because it was my first time ever in a prison.'

'There's always a first time. Prisons are for men,' said Umm Maher.

'You mean prisons are for Arabs,' said Abu Maher.

Mazen seemed to ignore his remark.

'The first two days were hell; they put us all in together.'

'All? Meaning?' I enquired.

'Arabs and Jews, drug dealers, drug addicts, criminals, Palestinian political activists, young and old. Once I realised that the great majority were Arab workers with no work permits like me I felt okay about it. But if I'm caught once more without a permit I'll be thrown in prison for three years. I've been sentenced in advance.'

'You've already been sentenced to three years for something you haven't done yet, for something you may do one day in your life? How efficient this Israel can be sometimes.' I found myself at a loss, frustrated and angry.

'Yes. I signed a paper promising never again to sneak into Israel for work, otherwise I get a three-year sentence.'

For a while I kept quiet, then I began asking questions like a tourist just arrived from Minnesota.

'Then why not apply for a work permit?'

'Are you kidding? They don't give us any. They don't want us anymore. They bring workers from all over the world: Taiwanese, Chinese, Ukrainians, Romanians, you name it, anyone but Palestinians.'

'But no one works as hard as we do,' mumbled Murad from under the sheet. Poor thing, he was still trying to get some sleep.

'You mean no one else is as cheap,' said Abu Maher.

With every negative note from Abu Maher, there was a positive note from Umm Maher.

'I bet you anything that no one, no one works as hard as Murad. I have nine sons, some older, some younger, but none of them can do the work he does. All his Yahoodi employers love him.' She was so proud of Murad she had tears in her eyes, as did I. Of course, we all knew how truly hardworking Murad was.

'He's a bulldozer,' interrupted Abu Maher, still immersed in his soap opera.

'Yes, a bulldozer, what's wrong with that?' objected Umm Maher.

As the two argued, my senses were becoming aroused by, and more interested in, the tantalising smells emanating from the nearby kitchen: fried eggs, fried goat's cheese and freshly baked whole wheat *taboun* bread. My attention shifted towards the colourful little plates placed on the round wicker tray carried by the sister. There were freshly cut tomatoes, slices of fragrant cucumber, big green olives and small black ones, pink and green pickles, spring onions, round balls of *labneh* dipped in dark olive oil, a plate of hot green and red peppers and the typical seasoned *za'tar* with roasted sesame seeds and sour sumac.

Umm Maher hopped up to help her daughter place the tray on the floor. I was starting to feel hungry again after overcoming my initial fear about my mission that night. I went back to my mattress and cushions. Trying to keep my balance, I sat with one leg bent and the other stuck close to my body in such a way so as to reach the fried eggs and white goat's cheese that luckily had been placed on the nearer half of the tray. I was resigned to the fact that I had no choice but to resist the delicious green and black olives placed on the further half of the round tray.

'Come and eat with us.' I found myself acting as the hostess.

'No, no thanks, I need to go back,' said Mazen.

'Why don't you eat with the doctora?' Umm Maher addressed her two sons.

'Mother, we just ate, we can't eat again,' said Mazen before leaving the room.

'Okay, fine . . . Doctora, why don't you and Mohammad eat and then try to get an hour or so of sleep? I'll wake you up at two-fifteen; a quarter of an hour before the Ford comes to pick you up. Is that enough time to get ready?'

Plenty, I thought, since I was planning to keep my rumpled appearance. I covered myself with a light blanket and finally shut my eyes. I was nowhere near being sleepy or asleep. Mohammad lay on a mattress with his head close to mine and Murad tossed on his mattress. Mazen had disappeared; probably back to the coffee shop since there was no prospect of work tomorrow, or in the foreseeable future. Meanwhile, Abu Maher quietly continued to watch the eight hundred years of Arab rule in Andalusia which meant eight hundred episodes, one a day for the eight hundred days to come, a never-ending Syrian soap opera similar to the American soap opera *Peyton Place*.

'Goodnight. Will get you up in an hour or so, let's say around two-fifteen? Mohammad, why don't you set the alarm on your mobile, just in case?' said Umm Maher.

Mohammad was snoring.

'Goodnight doctora.'

'Goodnight Umm Maher.'

I lay on my back staring at the semi-darkness of the high ceiling. With an architect's obsession, I was fixated on figuring out its exact height. I estimated probably three metres sixty. Like the rest of the walls, it hadn't been painted. The semi-smooth texture and the cement colour added to its austerity. From the middle of the ceiling a naked bulb dangled some forty centimetres down. The light was off.

On the opposite cement wall, above Murad, were a number of photographs. From the photographs hanging on this wall one could easily trace the history of photography (colour and technique), as well as the male history of the Subhi family. The only problem was that they had been hung way too high, probably at a height of three metres forty centimetres. This meant they were only twenty centimetres below the ceiling, and considering that the only light in the room was coming all the way from the Alhambra Palace in Granada, it was difficult to make out the details. Except for one black and white photograph of some great-great-great-grandmother, all the photographs were of men.

Since my adrenaline levels were still high, I continued with my architectural obsessions: on the wall to my right, above the sofa, was a gilded, three-dimensional tableau (almost a model) of the Dome of the Rock. This was so close to the ceiling that it almost touched the heavens.

Still unable to sleep, I lay there theorising: the thing that intrigued me most was how a relatively big room like this had only one tiny window. It had taken me a lifetime to understand why peasant houses, old and new, didn't have big windows overlooking beautiful views of splendid olive groves and fruit orchards (never mind the Israeli settlements for now). Could it be that the last thing peasants wanted when they came home, dead tired from working in the fields all day, tilling the land, planting, harvesting, picking and pressing olives, was to see those fields again? The closed, dark houses were about taking peasants away from the hot sunshine and dusty fields. Would I want a window overlooking my Riwaq office? I asked myself. Could it be that the very concept of a 'nice view' and 'enjoying nature' was an urban one?

It dawned on me how easy my life had been. Here I was in the middle of the night, lying on my back, carrying on with my hypothesis and analysis about vernacular architecture, which is what I'd been doing all my professional life, while Murad had to get up as early as two-thirty in the morning in order to make a living. At long last, my architectural analysis helped me to doze off.

I was the captain in charge of giving the Jewish workers permits to build a pork factory. My big office had a huge glass window over-looking a splendid park. In the park were thousands-of-years-old crooked olive trees, tall cypresses and huge oaks, all twenty or thirty metres high. I would give the Jewish settlers work permits only if they went out and cut down at least one of those historic trees. I needed to clear the area so as to be able to see the view which had been blocked for centuries. Every time a settler went out and cut a tree, I would watch from my big window, and I would grant him a work permit. I watched him run out happily, delighted that he now had a work permit which allowed him to work in the huge Palestinian embroidery factory in the town of Ramallah, which he couldn't easily reach because of the many checkpoints I had instructed the PDF (Palestinian Defence Forces) to set up between major Israeli towns and the settlement. The cutting down of trees went on until the settlers cleared them all and only then could I clearly see the view: the eight-metre-high concrete Wall.

With the settlers' work permits still in my hand I heard Umm Maher say, 'Suad . . . Suad . . . get up . . . get up . . . it's two-thirty already . . . I'm making the coffee. You wash your face and get ready . . . We all seem to have overslept . . . The Ford is outside waiting for you.'

Half-asleep, I jumped out of bed (just before having a chance to distribute the settlers' work permits), ran to the bathroom and splashed cold water on my sleepy face, which was marked with funny pillow lines. I fixed my cap, tucked my hair under it, put on my black sunglasses and my denim jacket and ran out.

'Here is your coffee,' said Umm Maher.

I took my coffee cup and stepped out into the garden. It was still dark so I removed the sunglasses. The smell of the lemon blossom, which blended nicely with the coffee aroma, filled my lungs. The donkey honked goodbye. The dog was still asleep. I placed the coffee cup on the low parapet in the garden and ran up the steep hill after Murad.

My heart was already pounding.

I was psychologically preparing myself, shifting roles from dream to reality.

5.

Good Morning, Palestine

Sunday 13, 2007 [2:45 AM]
From Mazare' in-Nobani to the
Village of Izzawiyyeh

Perhaps it was the serenity of the cold, crisp morning that made the bustle of the small and shabby Ford bus, which had just arrived to pick up the village workers, sound more like a military tank.

The utter silence of the partially sleepy village made Murad's few words, aimed at the bus driver, echo across the fruit orchard behind him. The bright orange of the vibrating vehicle echoed the obtrusive orange lights of the Israeli settlement on the other side of the valley. Anxious about being spotted by the Israeli army, how I wished that bus was a demure white.

The light shining out of the bus windows cast monstrous shadows onto the dirty, narrow road. The strong front beam of the bus struck someone's house and garden at an angle. The reflections on a window, the lustrous, roughly textured white limestone of the house and the playfulness of the shuddering light on a huge fig tree made it feel as if the bus were a spaceship just landed from outer space. The way these Ford buses drive in Palestine, day and night, trying to go around hundreds of Israeli checkpoints, over mounds of dirt and around cement blocks, down and up riverbeds, along rocky valleys and un-asphalted paths, all of this qualifies them, if not as spaceships, then at least as James Bond super cars. I know of many Palestinian children who, in the absence of an amusement park, ask their parents to take them on a ride in a Ford bus. And if there is anyone who deserves a world medal for resilience, patience and resistance against the Israeli occupation, it is Ford bus drivers.

The empty seats behind the driver, with his big head, thick black hair and navy blue shirt, made me realise that we were the first workers to be picked up. I looked around for Mohammad, my security blanket on this trip.

'Where did you go?' I asked.

'Maher's wife whispered to me as we were leaving and I ran upstairs to see what she wanted. She begged me to carry some stuffed vine leaves and aubergines she had cooked and packed securely for Maher. "Murad always refuses, would you take it for him? *Hazeet* (poor thing)," she said, "it's his favourite dish . . . he probably hasn't had a proper hot meal since he left almost a month ago. *Please* take it for him," she begged me, but I refused,' said Mohammad.

'You should've taken it. She would've felt good, and we could've eaten it on the way,' I said wistfully.

'Hurry up, we're late,' I heard Murad say as he got on the bus.

'Late for work we don't even have . . . yet.' I caught myself saying 'we'. I guess the bond had already been formed.

'We've got to get there before sunrise, so none of the soldiers can spot us,' Mohammad explained.

There . . . where? I wondered, but didn't ask as the night (or rather morning) was still young. I had promised myself to refrain from asking too many questions on this trip.

I was feeling more apprehensive about being with Palestinian workers than I had been about being with Jewish workers only a quarter of an hour earlier. At this early hour of the day, it wasn't clear to me what was more unreal: my dream or this reality. I stepped back to make sure that Mohammad got on the bus before me. Feeling a bit shy and inhibited, I followed.

'Good morning, Abu Abdallah,' Mohammad greeted the bus driver. Quietly, I did the same.

'Good morning,' answered the driver, first looking in the mirror, then twisting his head backwards so as to make sure that what he had seen was for real.

'I see we've got two new workers with us today.' He smiled. Feeling nervous, I ignored the very first reaction to having me on this trip. I had made the decision not to speak until someone insisted, and, even then, to try to leave it to Mohammad to handle. One thing I was sure of: I did not want to be a journalist on a trip. I had convinced myself that I would pass for a Palestinian male worker and did not want anyone to challenge me.

Nothing around me made sense; why should I?

Bending forward slightly, I walked to the very end of the bus to find myself a seat whose inner sponge fillings weren't bulging out of the grubby wine-red fabric. I went and hid in a window seat on the very last row. I could feel the iron springs under my cushion as I leaned backwards, sliding and sinking into my seat. Something about the way I contracted my body reminded me of my childhood schooldays in Amman. No matter how much I tried to shrink into the wooden bench, in a hopeless attempt to sit in the first row, being by far the tallest kid, sooner or later classmates would complain and the teacher would insist that I sit in the very last row, just as I did now.

Through the dusty glass, nose flattened, I saw the silhouettes of two men coming in our direction. As they reached

42

the bus and came under the high beam, my heart ached, and my anxiety about more reactions to my presence was amplified. Meanwhile, Mohammad had settled down next to me, while Murad, probably a bit embarrassed, sat in front. He was subtly distancing himself from his increasingly cool-looking brother and his brother's crazy boss.

The two young workers got on the bus.

'Good morning Abu Abdallah, morning Murad . . . Hey, morning Mohammad,' the first said, sounding excited. 'Morning,' said the second, in a softer voice.

'Good morning Ramzi . . . Good morning Saed,' replied the driver.

With each and every 'morning' I got an inquisitive and not so subtle look, but so far no comments. They were too shy to ask and I left it at that. One came closer to us, while the other settled next to Murad.

I was delighted that the driver was mentioning each of the worker's names. In order to handle their funny reactions and my discomfort, I kept myself busy with the impossible mission of remembering all of them. I've always been bad with names: Ramzi and Saed, Saed and Ramzi. I kept repeating and alternating their names to myself. Ramzi was the young and comical-looking boy, while Saed was the tall, good-looking young man. Ramzi was the one with funky white glasses, while Saed was the one with a harelip. Ramzi was the one with short black hair, and Saed was the one with the long, light brown wavy hair. Ramzi was this . . . and Saed was that . . . In short, Ramzi was the funny-looking boy and Saed was the handsome young man.

Ah . . . *Saed,* all of a sudden it hit me.

'Is this *the* Saed?' I asked Mohammad.

'Yes,' Mohammad answered in a low voice, giggling.

'Now I understand,' I replied. My interest in gossip made me almost miss out on the names of the newcomers.

'Good morning.' Three new workers got on the bus.

'Morning Abu Yousef. Good morning Majed.'

Abu Yousef, Abu Yousef, Abu Yousef,
Majed, Majed, Majed,
Abu Yousef and Majed . . . Majed and Abu Yousef.

One was Abu Yousef and one was Majed, but what about the third? Which one was Majed? And which one was Abu Yousef? Abu Yousef must have been the skinny old man, while Majed was the tall chubby young man. While I was concentrating on the third, whose name I had missed, four more workers got on the bus.

Okay, Suad, go easy on yourself. You still have a long way to go, and plenty of time to remember their names.

With every 'morning' I got a funny and curious glance. Some were better than others at hiding their shock.

'Morning Muneer.'

'Morning Musheer.'

Okay Suad, concentrate:

Muneer, Muneer, Muneer,
Musheer, Musheer, Musheer,
Shaheer, Shaheer, Shaheer.

Muneer, Musheer, Shaheer.

44

As more and more 'eers' got on the bus, I was soon at a loss as to who was who; they were all starting to look the same. I was trying hard to resist the fact that they all looked alike, only to learn later that the three 'eers' looked alike simply because they were brothers. Oh well.

The more workers got on the bus, the more difficult it became to spot me.

'Okay . . . we've got to move on, anybody missing from the eastern neighbourhood, *al-harah al-sharqiyyeh*?' asked Abu Abdallah the driver.

'Just go.' Someone sounded impatient.

Soon the bus came to a second stop and more workers got on. One after the other, 'Morning', '*Salam*', 'Morning', '*Assalamo 'alaikum*, peace be upon you', 'How are you, Abu Abdallah?', 'Morning', 'Why so late today?', 'No seats left?', 'Where shall we sit, on the floor?' Some squeezed themselves onto the seats, others sat on the floor, and two stood up, bent over. The crowdedness of the small bus made it almost impossible to keep count. Nevertheless, I gave it a try: we must have been a little less than two dozen. By now, of course, I had given up on the idea of memorising anybody's name.

Faceless illegal workers let it be.

6.

One Thousand and One Arabian Nights

Sunday May 13, 2007 [2:55 PM]
On the Bus: from Mazare' in-Nobani
to the Village of Izzawiyyeh

I tried to keep myself busy by looking out of the window, but the smeared and dusty glass didn't make it easy. I pulled the dark green curtains and squeezed them behind my back. I must admit, that filthy, sticky fabric really got to me. To reduce the claustrophobia caused by the hot flushes of an anxious, menopausal woman in a crowded, stuffy bus, I fiddled around with the knob of the window, trying, and failing, to open it.

I pressed my head against the window but all I could see was the reflection of my own face and Mohammad's shoulders. I tucked the dangling tufts of my hair into my cap and once again pressed my forehead even closer to the window. I framed my face with my two palms, in order to block out the inside light, and looked out. With difficulty I could, every now and then, spot an old peasant's stone house, or one of the newly constructed concrete boxes (supposedly functioning as houses). But the condensation of my breath on the glass made it almost impossible for me to see.

Once again, I reached for and jiggled the window knob. Mohammad helped to unlock it and slid the window wide open for me. I stuck my head out of the window; the cold, crisp air instantly cooled my sweaty face and my blushed cheeks. It was like quenching a burning hot surface with cold water. Now and then I could smell the appetising odour of the *taboun,* the burning bread ovens; the one smell that I adored in villages.

The narrow, unlit bumpy road took us back the same way that Mohammad and I had come from only a few hours earlier. I tried to orientate myself by spotting the coffee shop in the 'village plaza'. We soon passed its green painted wooden shutters and I could still smell the aroma of the many cups of coffee which the village *shabab*, the young men, had had as they watched the football match while their caffeine and adrenaline levels shot up.

Gradually, my eyes grew used to the darkness outside. In the midst of the dark, creepy gardens and olive groves I could spot a lit house every now and then, or a lit room in a house. Knowing it was too early for the dawn prayers, I wondered how many of the village mothers, wives and sisters had got up at this odd hour of the night in order to prepare the coffee and breakfast for the bread winner(s) of their families. I wondered if some diligent students were also up and about preparing for the final school exams which were due in June, less than a month away.

In the vicinity of the few lit houses, and from their silhou-ette and shapes, I was trying to guess if the trees were fig, almond, pine, walnut or olive. The easiest to guess were tall cypress trees which were often planted next to low rubble-stone walls demarcating, and separating, the adjacent *hawakeer* (fruit orchards) that could be found around every single peas-ant house.

Soon we were out of the village. There was complete silence; a darkness and eeriness outside that contrasted with the endless liveliness and animation inside: the non-stop joking and talking that I eventually twisted my body towards and tuned into.

It didn't take long before young, funny Ramzi, sitting only two rows away from us, looked at Mohammad, not at me, and said in a most hilarious tone, '*Amanet Allah*, honestly, is *she* coming with us?'

'She's also looking for work,' replied Mohammad.

There was a hysterical laughter all around. At that point most of the workers twisted their heads in different directions to really examine me. Having been recognised by everyone, I first blushed but then felt much more at ease. Now that the difficult part of being accepted on this trip was over, I started taking note of things around me in a much more relaxed way.

I took a deep breath, sat back and began eavesdropping.

'So, who won yesterday?' I heard someone ask.

'Qarawah, of course. They led by 8-2 in the first half, and scored 9 against 3 in the second.'

'If it hadn't been for that stupid referee, who waved four red cards and five yellow at our team, we would've won, but by the end we were left with only seven players.'

'Football?' I looked towards Mohammad and enquired. I wanted to be part of the conversation. And since I did watch football, once every four years, I could tell that eight goals before half time and nine after were a bit too much.

'Yes, football,' Mohammad replied dismissively, not realising that his boss's other talents included being a defender in the mixed football team for Ann Arbor City in 1978. If Mohammad had known the types of drills we women had to go through in order to receive that heavy ball on our not so flat chests he certainly wouldn't have been so dismissive on the subject.

Mohammad joined in with the stream of curses against that reckless referee.

'Why so many goals?' I asked.

'Why not? Didn't we win 8-0 against China in 2004?' Mohammad replied proudly, recalling a game our 'national' team played in Taiwan.

Sure, why not? I thought to myself. This is Palestine, after all. It is quantity not quality that counts. It was quantity that scared not only Taiwan, but also Israel, who, in March 2006 bombarded the football stadium in Gaza, leaving a massive crater in its centre. Israel had been so threatened by the Palestinian team winning the first match against Chinese Taipei (8-0) that it set out to prevent several members of the team from leaving Gaza. As a result of this vindictive act, Palestine lost its chance to qualify as World Cup contenders. If this act of jealousy had not been carried out by Israel then we Palestinians could perhaps have modestly been the world champions! Yes, we could even have won against our beloved Italy. You probably didn't know that we have an excellent record, winning against France in 1993 even though the French team included Michel Platini (not Zidane, thank God) and other world-famous players.

End of game.

'Ramzi . . . Saed . . . Majed, for God's sake stop smoking, the day hasn't started yet,' exclaimed the old man.

'Here, I'll open the window for you, Abu Yousef. Are you happy now?' replied Majed.

'I'd be happier if you stopped smoking altogether,' replied Abu Yousef.

'You wouldn't have complained if it was a *frameh*! Right, Abu Yousef?' asked Ramzi.

There was a big outburst of laughter.

'Whatever it is, stop smoking and shut that bloody window. It's freezing,' shouted one of the three 'eers' sitting next to Abu Yousef.

'*Hader,* right away, Muneer.'

Okay, Suad. So far, you've figured out that a *frameh* was probably marijuana or hash, the skinny, balding older man was Abu Yousef, and the stocky one sitting next to him was Muneer.

'Hey guys, have we forgotten Abu Ali?' someone from the front shouted.

'No, no, we haven't forgotten him, he left early this morning. He went to Jerusalem. He wanted to sneak around Qalandia checkpoint, his Yahoodi employer is waiting for him on the other side of the Wall.'

Earlier than this? was all I could think.

'It'll cost him at least a hundred and fifty shekels to sneak into Jerusalem around the Qalandia checkpoint.'

'A hundred and fifty shekels – forty-five dollars? Bloody hell, that's a whole day's pay, that's if you're lucky enough to find work the same day.'

'Yes, a hundred and fifty shekels, but he gets there for sure, not like us.'

'Sometimes you pay a hundred and fifty shekels in advance to the bus driver, who promises to sneak you in, but instead you get shot at and caught, in addition to losing all the money you have.'

'True, but in most cases the chances of sneaking in from Qalandia are much higher than from 'Azzoun Village.'

'You know why? Because Jerusalem Ford drivers bribe the Israeli soldiers. All it takes is to hand the soldier fifty shekels, or, even better, a *grooz* (twenty-pack carton) of cigarettes.'

'A *grooz*! You must be out of your mind. One pack of cigarettes, maximum two, would often do the job.'

'Best is *hashisheh,*' Ramzi broke out into deafening laughter. Everyone else followed suit. Not having someone else to tease, Ramzi moved closer to us, stared at me and then asked, 'Mohammad, what are you up to?'

'Me and *m'alimti* (my boss), doctora Suad, are looking for work like you. Please, if someone offers her a job, don't compete with her. Give her a chance. This is her first experience of looking for work. She's got to find a job right away,' Mohammad giggled.

Ramzi burst into squeaky laughter, like the young Mozart in *Amadeus*.

'No, really, Mohammad, what are you two up to?' Ramzi insisted.

'It is not right to beg on our backs, *ma bisir tishhato ala dhourna*, or to make money out of our misery,' yelled someone from the front seat.

'*Ya rafeeq*, Comrade Muneer . . . Would I, or my boss, do such a thing?' objected Mohammad, half-joking, half-serious.

'Everybody does these days,' replied Muneer, also only half-jokingly.

'On the contrary, Comrade, the doctora is going to publish a book about your life . . . your sufferings.'

'She'll need volumes and volumes,' I heard someone say.

I was rather insulted by Muneer's comment, but kept quiet. This made me reflect on the ethics of what I was doing. Having noticed my utter discomfort, Mohammad decided to ignore Muneer's remark and move on to a lighter topic.

'Me and my boss Suad are going to ask for Lily's hand. She is Murad's fiancée. We want to improve the family's offspring.'

'Yes, yes, certainly you must . . . you don't want a baby that, God forbid, looks like Murad,' said Saed, Murad's competition but also Murad's closest and best friend.

More laughter.

Murad looked back with his adorable subtle smile. He was still quiet.

'But she is Saed's fiancée,' said Muneer, who was trying to apologise in his own indirect way. I understood it to mean: no hard feelings.

'Murad is my best friend. He can have her,' said Saed confidently. Being so handsome he must have had many other admirers. And he was about to add one more. I glanced discreetly at him. He was dangerously handsome. He resembled an even handsomer version of Russell Crowe in the *Gladiator*.

I took a breath and looked out of the window. It was still dark.

'Where are we now?' I asked.

'Qarawah.'

'Ah . . . The enemy's village,' I said, a late attempt to join in the football debate. I rested my elbow against the window and my eyes followed a greyish-white line, more like a white band, which somehow separated the almost-black rolling hills from the graded grey sky that grew darker and darker as I looked up. I could also spot a few twinkling stars. I took a deep breath and sighed. Nature had always been my true safe haven in moments of disquiet, even on a moonless night like tonight.

As the bus engine rattled along winding roads, every now and then I would spot some faint white lights on the far hills indicating an Arab village, or strong orange lights indicating an Israeli settlement. Even though we were driving in the very heart of the West Bank, in theory 'Palestinian territory', orange seemed to reign. For some reason or other, there seemed to be more shining stars above Arab villages.

The Ramzi Show-off Show:

'Does anyone have a concrete offer of work?' I heard Ramzi ask.

'I do.'

'Me too.'

'Me three.'

'Fuck you all, I *don't* . ... I am so jealous . . . I really hope your employers never show up.'

'Men, behave,' I heard Abu Yousef say.

'My permit to work on a settlement is still valid. I can always call my Yahoodi boss and have him pick me up any time I want. But you know I'd rather work in Israel.'

The bragging went on.

'Why give yourself so much trouble? Just call him now.'

'I'll call him if we don't make it today.'

'Stop it, you bad omen.'

Right in front of me, Abu Yousef objected, 'I hate working in settlements. I'd rather work in Israel. Once I worked on a construction site in a settlement near Nablus. Whenever

I was in a bad mood, like today, I would think there would be no end to their occupation and as a result these settlements would remain Jewish. I would say "Damn you settlers" and would cut down on the amount of cement in the mixture. But whenever I was in a good mood and optimistic, I would say to myself *Ya walad*, man, no occupation lasts forever, one day the Israeli army will withdraw, the settlers will leave and these settlements will eventually become ours. At that point I would pour more and more cement to make these houses last forever.'

'But Abu Yousef, what would happen if the houses with less cement became ours?'

'*Akalna hawa,* we'd be fucked,' replied Abu Yousef, laughing.

For the first time Saed made an effort to tell me a story:

'Murad and I worked in a club once. One day we arrived late to work. Each like a frantic rocket, *saroukh,* we started cleaning the huge conference hall. We dusted the tables and chairs, swept the floors spotlessly clean and organised everything nicely. But people started coming in while we were still doing the final touches. Our boss was so mad at us, he asked us to stop everything and leave the conference hall at once. So we did.

An hour or so later, we went out and bought some sardines, some mortadella salami and some bread, and finally sat down on the *desheh* (Hebrew word for a lawn) in the garden to eat. Before we'd even touched our food, we heard screams and the security alarm. Soon the well-dressed businessmen were dashing out of the conference hall. There was chaos and fear everywhere. When we enquired we were told that

54

the security men had spotted two suspicious brown bags in one corner of the conference hall. Murad and I looked at one another and nervously smiled; at that point we realised what had happened to our lunch bags which we had looked for everywhere. We were too embarrassed to admit to it.

Realising how much fear and chaos my mother's cheese sandwiches, dried figs and oranges had caused, we decided to sit back and simply watch from a distance as more and more . . . and more security men and experts were brought to the site. There were firemen everywhere, soldiers, police, border police and ambulances.

Soon a robot also arrived, and we both peered through the windows to watch. The room was filled with security experts who carefully cleared the way for the robot, the robot was switched on and was left to walk like this . . .' From his jammed seat, Saed imitated the mechanical walk of the robot.

'It walked in the direction of my mother's sandwiches, carefully picked the bags up and one by one placed them on the floor in the middle of the room, then BOOM! It pressed together its two mechanical hands and there was a big explosion. Don't ask me where the noise came from but believe me there were little bits of cheese here and there, there were little sticky pieces of dried figs and orange juice on the floor, there were shards of glass everywhere, there were shards of furniture everywhere, there was shredded paper everywhere, and finally the lights went off. An hour or so later everyone else went home and only Murad and I stayed behind cleaning up while starving to death.'

Intermission.

★　　★　　★

To take a break from the one thousand and one Arabian workers' nights, I took a deep breath and once more gazed out of the window. To my surprise, it was still dark. I looked at my watch and it was ten past three in the morning. After a forty-minute drive, I finally felt as if I was one of them and decided not to be hostage to their (especially Ramzi's) never-ending stories. It was such a relief to feel there was no longer any need to concentrate on what was being said around me. It had become silly and taxing. I didn't want to be the journalist on this trip, but so far they had treated me like one. I was adamant I'd put a stop to it.

I purposely turned my back away. From the misty window I watched the world, the dark world, go by.

I could still pick up bits and pieces of conversations in the background. Right in front of me, I overheard a juicy conversation:

'I say take it out of there, they search the mobiles.' I wondered what *it* was, perhaps a piece of hash.

'No they don't.'

'Give them a sexy photo of Nancy 'Ajram (the famous female Lebanese singer), they adore her. The other day a soldier arrested me and told me he would let me go if I sang him a Nancy 'Ajram song. I sang him *Ah o nus* ('Yes and a Half') and the soldier said, "Even though your voice is really terrible, I'll let you go".'

'You should have sung Haifa Wahbeh's* *Boos al-wawa* ('Kiss the Wound'). They love that even more.'

'The other day a soldier asked me if I had her on my mobile and asked me to SMS it for him, which I did.'

* A female Lebanese singer and famous sex symbol in the Arab world.

56

'The best is George Wassouf*. They love the guy.'

'You know why they love him? Because he's always stoned like most of them.'

The bus became much more animated once there was talk of fun topics such as sexy Lebanese singers and being stoned. I knew Beirut was always a source of fun for Arabs but I didn't realise it was for the Israeli soldiers as well. Only now did it occur to me why the Israeli soldiers stayed in Lebanon for twenty-two years (1982–2004); with so much hashish around, why would they leave. Even if they'd wanted to, they were probably so high they would have lost their way back.

I regained interest in the conversation. At this point Abu Yousef was feeling joyful, and this encouraged Ramzi:

'Mohammad . . . You know the story of your brother, Maher?'

For sure, Mohammad must've known the story of his own brother, but Ramzi nevertheless carried on.

'The Yahoodi who employed Maher was simple and dumb. After picking Maher up from Segula†, he drove him home and asked him to spray the trees in his garden with a chemical insecticide. But Maher didn't want to get poisoned, or to get cancer. After going around checking all the trees, Maher looked at the first tree and told the Yahoodi that this tree has diabetes and he must get rid of it; this one has high blood pressure, we must cut it down; this one is seriously ill, the leaves have cancer and we must cut it down. The guy believed everything Maher said. Maher then claimed he was

---

* A male Lebanese singer with a deep voice.
† One of Petah Tikva's industrial areas.

feeling very tired and sick that day, but he promised he would come back some other day to cut down the trees. Of course the Yahoodi never saw Maher's face again.'

'Poor old man, he believed everything Maher told him.'

I was really curious to know what that Israeli employer would have had to say about the dumb Arab worker he had picked up that day.

There was a few minutes break before the Ramzi Show continued:

'Are you spending the night on the construction site or in the open fields with Murad? Or, even better, in the *'abbarah* (the water tunnel under the highway), where Muneer and his brothers sleep?' Ramzi challenged us.

'No, better come and see *al-hursh* (the small woodland) area where we sleep. There are big mice, snakes, scorpions, you name it, it's a zoo and we're its monkeys,' added Majed.

'You're of course welcome to the water well where Majed and I sleep. No water, no electricity, no bath, no toilet; it's like the Stone Age.'

'You should see how terrible we look at the end of the night.'

'Look or smell?'

'Enough . . . enough . . . Hey guys, don't go overboard, people have their dignity, okay.' There were a number of objections and an uneasy silence.

'Stop it, guys, and start collecting ten shekels each. No need to delay the driver,' said Abu Yousef.

'Where are we now?' I asked, beginning to get a bit apprehensive about the new phase of our endeavour.

'We're in Izzawiyyeh Village.'

★   ★   ★

58

I stretched, in preparation for the long walk. Everyone stood up. Some of the men got off the bus while Abu Yousef said, 'I've been worried about walking in the olive groves since Friday.'

'How long have you been working in Israel?' I asked Abu Yousef as I got closer to him.

'Twenty-eight years,' he replied proudly.

'Twenty-eight years and you still worry?'

'It only gets worse, and we're not getting any younger,' he said as he stepped off the bus.

I was relieved to hear that someone other than me had been worried about this trip.

'Let's get going,' pushed one of the workers.

'*Ya Allah*, God, may you make it easy on us.'

'May God make our day fruitful.'

'*Ya Allah*, all of you say: *la illa-ha illa Allah* (there is no God but one God).'

'Hey . . . that's enough, you sound like Omar al-Mukhtar.'*

'You sound like an imam at Friday prayer.'

'Come on, guys, let's go,' insisted the same worker.

'Have you all paid?' asked Abu Yousef.

'Are we to walk all the way now?' I enquired.

'Yes, if all goes well we'll walk until we get to Kufur Qasem.'†

'How long?' I insisted.

'Two to three hours, if everyone walks fast and all goes well.'

---

* Omar al-Mukhtar (1862–1931), teacher of the Quran by profession, who became the leader of the Libyan resistance against the Italian occupation in 1912.
† An Arab village within Israel.

'Who is the slowest? I want to keep him company,' I said, joking, but of course was damn serious.

'Then don't walk with the two rockets, Murad and Saed, walk with the elders: Abu Yousef and Comrade Muneer. They're the slowest.'

I looked around, trying to grasp where we were. It looked like we had just landed in an out-of-place space. With a little left turn, the semi-asphalted road ended in a vast open area, a dirty parking lot where there were hundreds of parked cars and buses, some even shabbier than ours. The high beam of our bus on the old and dusty cars made me realise that some of these vehicles must've been left there for days, weeks or even months. A shiver ran down my spine. Would I ever come back? A moment of fear got hold of me. This vast car dump felt eerie. To the far left I could see olive countryside, to the right the narrow and winding road continued.

In the distance, a mile or two away, I could see some sort of pale, glowing light. The high dirt mounds, the barbed wire spotted with hundreds of black plastic bags, and the tens of cement cubes indicated that there was an Israeli checkpoint on the horizon. Before I had turned my back to it, I spotted a high concrete watchtower. I hoped, like 'Atara's checkpoint, that it had been left unattended, that it was only a daytime harassment point.

The vanishing rattle of our bus made me realise that there was no turning back on this trip.

7.

Night Hunters

Sunday May 13, 2007 [3:15 AM]

From Izzawiyyeh to Izzawiyyeh:*

From One Angle to Another

My late mother's husky voice echoed in my ears as I watched the workers being swiftly swallowed by the darkness of the olive groves one . . . by . . . one . . . *Susu, sweetie, there is nothing to be afraid of; darkness has no ghosts, and eats no one.* At which point I buttoned up my jacket, tucked my hair under my cap and briskly followed.

I was the last to surrender.

It took a while before I felt confident walking on the narrow, rocky path that wound down the hill between huge olives trees. Contrary to what Mum had said, the darkness did have ghosts. Making sure not to fall down or twist my ankle (and become an even heavier burden on Mohammad and Murad), I carefully placed my feet in semi-dark spots, and stopped every so often and took a deep breath, captivated by the sense of being surrounded by all the shapes and sizes of centuries-old ghosts, a few of which were Roman.

Walk . . . Walk . . . Walk . . . Stride . . . Stride . . . Stride . . .

★   ★   ★

* Izzawiyyeh is the name of a village but in Arabic it literally means 'an angle'.

61

The muezzin's call to prayer from the nearby village of Izzawiyyeh, as well as the thumping of the workers' boots, made it difficult for me to follow what was being said or argued. I was no longer a part of the conversations around me. The amplified noises echoed in the surrounding deep valley. The collective warmth of the bus was slowly being replaced by a strong sense of discomfort, loneliness and estrangement.

The more I stared at the mysterious landscape around me, the more I seemed to awaken the ghouls inside me, and this I wanted to bring to a halt instantly: so I stopped and deliberately initiated a dialogue with Mohammad.

'Now I understand why Abu Yousef has been worried about walking in the darkness of the olive groves since Friday . . . And it only gets worse, he said earlier.'

'It only gets worse . . . and it only gets worse,' I mumbled as I bounced down the rocky path. But soon I discovered that my repetitive mumblings of 'it only gets worse' were not echoed by the ghosts around me, but by Abu Yousef himself, who, I discovered, was walking right in front of Mohammad and me.

'No, doctora, it is not *this* darkness that worried me, it is the darkness in their hearts.'

'For God's sake, keep quiet, don't make so much noise, otherwise the soldiers will spot us. Soon you'll have to switch your mobiles off,' I heard someone say.

'How can Maher reach us or know where we are if I switch off my mobile phone?' Like many others, Mohammad objected.

'Walk faster, I tell you; if we don't manage to cross the barbed fence before sunrise, the soldiers will see us, none of us will make it and the day will be totally wasted.' The soldiers must be deaf not to hear us, I thought, but kept it to myself.

Abu Yousef's words helped me get over my childish fear of walking in a moonless night. I soon resumed my conversation with him.

'*Twenty-eight* years of work in Israel, and they refuse to even give you a work permit! Wow! By now you deserve a passport, not a work permit.'

'A PASSPORT! You must be kidding. They have no mercy and they know no God, what else can I say?' Abu Yousef paused for a moment, sighed, and continued,

'I spent my whole life working for them, and now look at me; like a thief, I steal my livelihood in the dark, *basruq 'ishti sirqa*. It used to take us half an hour to drive there, and now, as you see, it takes us a whole night in the hills . . . that's if we don't get arrested or beaten up.'

Arrested or beaten up! His words reminded me of the different possibilities still awaiting us. His words also made me recall last night's 'only once' conversation with Abu Maher.

Walk . . . Walk . . . Walk . . . Stride . . . Stride . . . Stride . . . Hardly any breath left.

The more we walked, the more I could see or imagine my surroundings: the two low rubble-stone walls which marked the sides of our crooked path, the terraced olive groves and the high rubble-stone walls which we had to jump every now and then. I could hear the tumbling stones behind the not so elegant walkers like myself. The fluffy, tilled dark-red earth looked black now.

63

I was very aware of the many small wild flowers, the poppies, tiny wild orchids, anemones, blue and white crocuses on which we were probably stepping; of the scared gazelles and hyenas running away from the night hunters; of the small stones on the ground beneath us; and, finally, of Mohammad's shoulders which acted as my walking sticks. It was on this trip that I realised, more than ever, that losing ten kilos was no more a personal choice but a national duty, if not for my sake then at the very least for the sake of the workers.

With the mysteriousness of darkness and the growing level of noise, I was becoming increasingly apprehensive that some cat-eyed soldier might spot us and shoot at us (meaning, shoot *me*), beat us up (meaning, beat *me* up) or arrest us (meaning, arrest *me*). While I was contemplating which one I would be subjected to tonight, my three-option hallucinations of a shooting, a beating and an arrest came to an end as I heard someone swear out loud, 'Oh *no* . . . Oh *fuck* . . . you son of a bitch.'

I suspected it was Murad.

I froze, listened, and fearfully examined all that surrounded me: suddenly there were hundreds and hundreds of dark silhouettes. There were ghosts here, there were ghosts there, there were ghosts *everywhere*.

Some appeared from behind ghostly olive trees.

Some were still winding along narrow paths.

Some sat under trees, some rested on black rocks, some leaned against rubble walls, and some dotted both sides of our path.

Some were in fast motion, some in slow.

Some animated, others suspended.

64

Some were small, some were gigantic.

Some with hoods, most without.

Some with masks, a few without.

Some hovered in large groups, some in small, some in pairs, a few alone.

Some seemed motivated, others seemed aimless.

Some were full of life, others seemed lifeless.

Some looked purposeful and others seemed purposeless.

Some were talking, others were silent.

My head was spinning, my body turning and my fear mounting. I was terrified and, for a fraction of a second I sensed the darkness seeping into my heart. I got hold of my senses, closed my eyes and listened: some spoke Palestinian Arabic with a few Hebrew words; others spoke Moroccan Arabic or Berber with French words; some spoke Turkish with German expressions; and some spoke Mexican Spanish with much American slang.

And some, like me, felt no need for words.

I stood there and wondered:

Was it a carnival of existence or a carnival for survival?

Was it a dance for life or a masquerade of death?

Was it for real or was it a vision?

Once I got rid of my fears and the black spot in my heart I figured out what it was: an innocent Saturday evening chase for a living.

A Night Hunters' outing.

I stood there and wondered:

Were they the hunters? Or were they being hunted?

Were they haunting or being haunted?

Were they the seekers or the sought after?

★　　★　　★

'What's going on, Mohammad?' I enquired.

'Don't know.'

'It's the army, *al-jaysh*,' I heard someone say.

'The bloody army.'

My heart skipped once . . . skipped twice . . . skipped a third time, then stopped.

'Oh . . . no, here's an Israeli jeep waiting for us,' said Abu Yousef in a tone that was desperate and slow.

'Where? Where?' Mohammad and I asked anxiously at exactly the same moment.

'Are they close? I can't see them,' I said, terrified.

'No . . . they're on the opposite hill,' assured Abu Yousef.

'Thank God.' The soldiers weren't close enough to arrest us or beat us up. I was so relieved to know that the only option left to them was to shoot at us. Once I was reassured that my book was not about to end on chapter five, I was happy to finally get some real action into this book.

'Do you see the blue neon light over there?' asked Muneer.

'No, where?' I replied as I concentrated on the different-coloured lights resembling stars in the semi-darkness. Across the highway, on the opposite side, I could see a line of white lights spotting the silhouettes of an Israeli settlement. The three or four huge orange floodlights were obviously for protection against 'the coming of the barbarians'.

Meanwhile, Abu Yousef continued, 'Okay, Suad, do you see the highway?'

'Yes.'

'A hundred metres or so across the highway to the left?'

'Yes, yes, I see the glittering blue neon right there. What is it?'

'It is the computer inside the Israeli military jeep.'

'Oh, I see.'

'The bastards *al-'arsat* have been here since two-thirty, so no one could pass,' I heard someone complain.

'We've been here since one-thirty; so far, no one has managed to pass,' said another worker from another group

'Fuck them; fuck their mothers.' Another angry contribution.

'*Kiss em abukum 'ars*,' I repeated the same curse but in a more gender sensitive form, targeting their fathers. I said it in a very, very low voice. Mohammad laughed.

'We could've slept a bit more.' I joked with Mohammad who giggled once more. 'What now?' I asked.

'We've got to wait until the bloody jeep goes away,' said Saed as he looked at Murad and asked, 'Murad, what do you say? Shall we go, like last time, on the side of the road, then in the tunnel under the highway?'

Oh no, we are not doing Victor Hugo's *Les Miserables,* I thought, realising that this was no longer a picnic in the olive groves.

'Let's just wait a bit, they'll probably leave soon,' I heard someone suggest.

'No, they're here to stay. What do you say, Murad?'

Before I knew it, Murad was on the run: like a fox he descended the uneven path, hopping from one rock to another. Realising that Murad knew best, everyone followed. I held onto Mohammad's shoulder and tumbled down as fast as I could. Down the hill, along the concrete side of the ditch, into the ditch, up the slanted side of the ditch and soon we were standing against the metal barrier on our side of the highway. At that point I looked back and realised that we were being followed by hundreds of other workers from other villages. They looked like monkeys hopping in all directions.

'Let's all cross the highway and go in different directions, then they can't possibly run after us.'

For the first time ever I felt that actions could be faster than words.

Everyone ran across the highway at different angles, over the concrete strip dividing the highway and across to the other side. Yes, the same side where the blue light in the jeep beckoned. There was chaos, there was noise, there were screams, there was laughter, but there were also shots in the dark. In a split second we were running back exactly the same way, to where we had been only a few minutes before. While taking a long deep breath I heard Murad say, 'Let's give it another try. Don't be scared, they're firing in the air.'

'They say six or seven workers from Bedia made it to the opposite hill. They either got away, *nafadu*, or they got arrested, *enmasaku*.'

Got arrested! It sounded so matter-of-fact. No one except me seemed to want to know what exactly had happened to these workers.

'Okay, let's give it another try, let's go,' said Saed, who almost always stood next to Murad. They were like inseparable twins; galloping next to one another like two good Arabian horses.

We ran west one more time, a few shouts in distorted Arabic this time: '*Irja!*', go back. This time we took orders from a real authority and ran back as instructed in a language that all workers, except for me, understood well. We ran a third time, and with every round we seemed to come back missing a few workers. No one knew or bothered to find out whether they were *nafadu* or *inmasaku*. It was not until the fourth hopeless round that an alternative strategy was finally adopted.

The more we ran the more energetic I became, and the higher my adrenaline the more courageous I became. All I knew was that in the new strategy, and in the new narrow path along the ditch, I was fourth in line. Yes, no longer the last one dragging behind. The high edge of the ditch, running along the highway, gave me the confidence required to be fourth in line. There was Majed, there was Saed, there was Murad and, believe it or not, there was me. Yes, I was fourth in line, and my security blanket Mohammad wasn't behind me. Mohammad had discovered a new talent on this trip: he was the photographer. As we stood in the darkness of the highway, he remembered that he could document this trip on his mobile phone. And thanks to him there is a shaky video documentary of our journey.

All was quiet except for the workers' steps trailing right behind me and the whizzing noise of the passing cars which were increasing in number as morning crept closer. The level of the highway, to our right, reached the heads of the short ones and the shoulders of the tall ones. This meant that while Murad could walk with his body erect, both Majed and Saed had to slightly bend their heads, while I walked half-bent over: not because I was the tallest, but because I was afraid of being spotted by the soldiers standing next to the military jeep on the other side of the highway.

The new strategy was to walk a kilometre or two along this ditch until we reached the *'abbarah* (the water tunnel under the highway). If we managed to cross the 'abbarah it meant that we would end up on the soldiers' side of the tunnel, but much further south. As long as we were not spotted or caught then the probability of getting to work on time would be quite good. Even if Murad hadn't explained his scheme, having a strategic mind I had already figured it out by myself.

I was closely and carefully watching the manner in which Murad was walking in the half-metre-wide drainage ditch. He was as quick as a gazelle, as alert as a fox and as patient as a camel. Being right behind him once more, I noticed how small and skinny this Murad was. I kept myself entertained by watching his Charlie Chaplin movements: his two feet at a wide angle, his stiff body, his jerky movements, his below-the-knee pants, and even his leather shoes. Everything about Murad somehow reminded me of my adored Charlie Chaplin. Only his spiky hair looked more like Bart Simpson's.

While busy combining Charlie Chaplin with Bart, I heard Majed whisper to Murad, 'Look, look, look, there are two soldiers on the opposite hill, over there . . . over there.' Majed bent his head down, as did Murad, but I – as the Italians say – was *a terra*.

When I looked up, Majed was still stretching his arm and pointing towards the suspected images of soldiers.

'I can't figure out whether they're bushes or soldiers,' said Majed. But Murad didn't seem to worry; he gave a hand gesture meaning just to carry on. Majed continued walking. Saed, myself and everyone else behind me followed suit.

By now the early morning light was breaking. I could see shades and shadows. I not only spotted the two soldiers and made out a third, a fourth . . . but in no time I saw a whole regiment. Some were hiding behind bushes and boulders, pointing their rifles in our direction; others were standing still, pointing their Uzis in the opposite direction; some were flat on their tummies; but most were frantically spinning while mutely shooting in every direction.

Recalling how the Israelis and the Americans had their own interpretation of Newton's theory; that 'for every action there is a reaction, in all directions, and a hundred times as strong', which they'd applied in all their wars against us (in the 1948 ethnic cleansing, in the 1967 ongoing occupation, and in the present battle of impoverishment), and not wanting to risk getting into a big battle, for Murad's sake, I kept a low profile.

Walk . . . Walk . . . Walk . . . Stride . . . Stride . . . Stride . . . A long and deep breath.

But that ongoing rhythm was soon broken by a scream from Majed, and Murad turning around swiftly. I heard Majed beg, 'For God's sake, don't shoot, *mshan allah ma tukh*,' as he put his two arms up in surrender. Having used his mother tongue, Arabic, and not Hebrew, I realised the gravity of the situation. My heart skipped a few beats before I turned and followed Murad, who was running away as fast as a bullet. I, like the others, understood that the minute Murad ran that fast there was real danger.

Like a cannonball, I ran along in a zigzag motion, bouncing between the slanted left side of the ditch and the rocky right side. It wasn't easy to keep my balance in fifty or sixty centimetres of ditch filled with puddles here and there. When we got to safe ground I looked behind, but there was no one. Once more I was in the exact same spot that we had been in only some thirty minutes earlier.

The same feelings of anger and frustration I'd had as a little girl playing Snakes and Ladders with my brother and friends took hold of me. Every time I thought I'd reached the end of the board, a monstrous venomous snake would spring up at me, forcing me to slip down a ladder, which took me back, again and again, to the exact same spot where I'd first begun.

Not taking my heavy breathing into account, I must have broken a world record but, as so often happened in Palestine, there were no international referees to witness what was happening.

8.

Nothing to Lose But Your Life

Sunday May 13, 2007 [3:45 PM]
From Izzawiyyeh to Izzawiyyeh:
Once Again from One Angle to Another

When the dust settled from this round Majed was missing.

'Where is Majed?' I asked.

'Probably arrested by the two soldiers, that's why he put his arms up in surrender and that's when Murad ran like a bullet,' explained Muneer, who, like most comrades, had a tendency to over-explain the obvious. What bothered me most was that he was elaborating as if I wasn't there.

'Ramzi, why don't you call him and find out what happened to him?' asked Muneer.

'I already did, no reply,' answered Ramzi. End of conversation, no big fuss, life goes on.

'Bastards, they were waiting for us on *our* side of the ditch,' said Ramzi. Thank God they saved us the scary walk under the tunnel. That was all I could think of.

'I told you we'd better wait until they go away. It's too late now, the sun has already risen and they'll see us. Our only chance is to wait until they go away.'

'They're here to stay, *finito*, the day is burnt, no contractors will pick us up for work this late in the day.'

I looked at my watch; it was five-thirty in the morning.

'Let's get a fire going, it's cold,' complained Ramzi.

Since I was burning on the inside and sweating on the

73

outside, I didn't understand why Ramzi would want to start a fire. Anyway, nothing Ramzi had said or done on this trip had made much sense, so why should it now? Also, since they weren't out of shape, or menopausal, they probably needed a fire. Some of the men went around fetching sticks for the fire, some were yawning, others restlessly strolling back and forth, while the majority stretched out on rocks here and there.

'Can't get the fire started, sticks are wet,' complained Ramzi.

'Keep at it, it'll light eventually,' suggested Muneer.

By starting a fire I understood that the workers had given up on not being seen by the soldiers. In actuality, by now there was enough light for the jeep to spot us and for us to clearly see it. The hide-and-seek, or the workers' hunting in the dark, was over. From now on all of the action would take place under the bright May sun.

We had no option but to sit around and wait.

I sat on a flat rock, stretched my legs and joyfully watched the breaking of the soft morning light. The sky was turning a beautiful light pink and greyish blue. The huge olive trees, mostly on our side, were changing from a dark brown to a dark silvery green. For the first time since we started, I could see the white limestone rocks mushrooming from the tilled red soil. In the distance were beautiful formations of huge, dark grey boulders which formed a small cliff that dropped towards the highway.

Even though it was a cool May, with the exception of the bright yellow of the Spanish broom, the dark green thyme and the sage bushes, most of the wild flowers and bushes had dried up, particularly the wild thistles. The opposite hill, where the army stood, was spotted only with shrubs, since most of the olive trees had been 'cleared' to make way for the new settlements whose lights were still glowing.

For the first time I could clearly see the jeep on the other side of the highway, parked in a cleared piece of land. Its glittering blue neon light looked less eerie now. Finally I saw the three soldiers standing right under a glowing electrical pole. The strong orange spots made them look like actors on a stage, their huge Uzi machine guns twinkling with little stars. Wow, how much safer it felt to see three soldiers in the spotlight than to imagine a whole regiment in the dark.

My companions' activities around me made me realise that we would probably be here for quite a while. I rose from my seat on the rock and settled under a nearby olive tree. I rested my back on its centuries-old trunk, stretched my long aching legs in front of me and watched the workers go by.

There were workers everywhere, and the thing that drew my attention most was their village or sub-village groupings. They sat around fires or rocks in groups, they walked in groups, they talked in groups, they ate in groups and they played cards in groups. Some were truly old and others were truly young, but most of them were Murad's age, twenty to twenty-five: not surprising, knowing that seventy-five percent of Palestine's population was under twenty-three years of age. Two of the workers touched my heart. They were my age or even older: one was frail, the other with an apparent limp. I thought of what I had done and how much I had when I was in my twenties, studying, living it up, enjoying every aspect of a glamorous city like Beirut in the early seventies.

'So what is it *exactly* that you're doing here?' enquired a young boy in red. I somehow had noticed him earlier. He, like many others, had been staring at me for some time. He abandoned his village group and came closer to ours. There were workers from seven or eight different villages sitting around fires, eating or playing cards. The boy-in-red must have been the youngest among them all. He must've been thirteen years old, maybe fourteen at most. Our young Ramzi looked old in comparison.

'She's working on a book.' I could hear Ramzi's laughter from around the fire.

'A book!' exclaimed the young boy-in-red, rather astonished.

'Ya, she is documenting our pains.'

'Workers of the world unite; you have nothing to lose but your chains,' said Comrade Muneer, who else?

'Workers of Palestine, forgive us, *samahouna,* you've nothing to lose but your lives,' said Abu Yousef cynically.

The boy-in-red was way too young to understand the political reference. He simply carried on, 'No really, why are you here?'

'I'm writing a book,' I confessed. My words sounded ridiculous even to me. Never in my life had I felt so guilty and so silly being a writer. This boy made me feel ashamed of myself and of my writing.

'No, I'm kidding, I am like you, in search of a job in Israel,' I rephrased my answer.

'He will believe her only when he gets a copy of her book,' said Mohammad, directing his mobile-camera at the boy.

'That's assuming he knows how to read and write,' said Ramzi.

It was amusing the way they talked about me in the third person. It seemed to be common practice when referring to children and women; so much for my attempt to look like one of the Big Boys.

'Of course I know how to read and write. I left school at fifth grade, I had to accompany my father to work in Israel,' the boy responded to Ramzi's accusations.

'And where is your father?' I asked the boy, who by now was sitting very close to me. I somehow felt he needed a protective father on this trip, and he must have felt he needed a protective mother too. I moved a bit closer to him. He smiled.

'My father swore not to ever, ever work in Israel. Never again, he says.'

'Why not?' I asked inquisitively.

'For the last three times, he worked, but never got paid. He discovered that his Israeli employer had reported him to the police. Each time he made him work for a whole month, and then behind his back he would report him to the police, who would arrest him just before he managed to collect his money.'

'Hey, kid, don't exaggerate, she is not a reporter for Al Jazeera TV. Don't listen to him. Israeli employers are a hundred times better than Arabs,' I heard someone from behind say.

'Fuck them all, they're no better, they just pay more,' said Abu Yousef.

'It amounts to the same thing, doesn't it?' said Muneer.

'More than once my Yahoodi boss hid me away from the border police. So did the Yahoodi mechanic the other day when the border police arrested workers and beat the hell out of them.'

While the big village boys carried on with their comparative stories, the small boy-in-red sulked and spoke no more. I felt like hugging him tightly, but of course I couldn't. Since I was adamant there would be no tears on this trip, with a pretend cheerfulness I asked, 'So where are you from?'

'I'm from the village of Farkheh,' he replied, his eyes lighting up again.

'You're from where?' I enquired again, totally confused.

'Yes, yes, he is from a chicken, you heard him correctly,' joked Ramzi from a distance. I was wondering to myself why a village would be called Farkheh, which meant chicken in Arabic.

'I'm from a chicken,' replied the boy.

'The smart peasants called their village 'chicken' so as to deceive the Israeli settlers. Who would want to steal a chicken, after all?'

Once again Ramzi managed another round of making fun of the boy.

'Look, look, look, over there, under the big tree, there are soldiers with six or seven arrested workers,' I heard someone say from a distance.

I stood up, and sure enough I could see a few workers kneeling down with two soldiers standing next to them, one pointing his rifle close to a worker's head.

'See that, Mohammad?' I asked.

Mohammad was still playing around with his phone-camera when two workers approached him, and one furiously said, 'Hey, you, don't take my photo . . . do you understand? I tell you, don't take my photo,' he repeated.

'Okay . . . okay, cool it, man, this is not for Al Jazeera, okay.'

'I don't give a fuck who it's for, all I know is that I don't want my photograph taken . . . Otherwise . . .'

'Otherwise what?' asked Mohammad. 'Are you threatening me?' All of a sudden I saw a new side to Mohammad.

'Hey . . . hey, Abu Laban . . . Stop it . . . stop it . . . this is Murad's brother, Mohammad . . . No risk, no danger. Okay.'

'Ah . . . you should have told me you're Murad's brother,' one of them gently tapped Mohammad on the shoulder, while the other retreated two steps back.

'I am *matloub,* that's why I have to be careful,' said the taller one.

'You're wanted and you're sneaking into Israel for work!' exclaimed Mohammad.

'What stupidity,' Mohammad whispered in my ear, adding, 'He is probably from *Kataeb al-Aqsa,* the Fatah military wing.'

Realising the need to lighten up, Ramzi commenced his show once more:

'Doctora, do you know how many kids Abu Yousef has?' Before I had a chance to tune in to Ramzi's show, he replied, 'Twelve . . . and a new one on the way.'

It wasn't easy for me to shift gears, and moods, that quickly. I was still thinking of the wanted guy and the paradox of sneaking into Israel for safety. It was safer for some of them in Israel than in their own villages in the West Bank.

'Abu Yousef probably does not know about the baby on the way,' Ramzi added.

'God damn . . . fuck off, Ramzi,' replied Abu Yousef from around the fire. Everyone was laughing and yelling, including myself.

'He's sixty with a new baby on the way,' said Basheer.

'Abu Yousef . . . How old are you?' I asked.

79

'Forty-one,' he replied, smiling distantly.

'No way,' I found myself saying.

'Come here, Abu Yousef, they want to interview you for Al Jazeera,' said Ramzi.

'He has no teeth, that's why he looks so old, poor thing,' said Basheer.

'He's younger than me,' said Muneer. 'I'm forty-four and he is two or even three years younger than me.'

'No, truly, Abu Yousef, how old are you? And how many kids do you have?'

Both Ramzi and Basheer were acting like TV reporters. Neither Mohammad nor I intervened.

'Only ten,' he said.

'*Only*! Oh, poor thing.'

'Like an army of locusts . . . and who feeds that army of locusts?'

'God takes care of all.'

'Ya, God opens a bank account for each one of them the day they pop out from their mother's womb; right, Abu Yousef?'

'Ya, in the Israeli Bank of Hapoalim, which he can't get to because he has no permit.'

'You know, Abu Yousef, if you were an Israeli citizen you would've made a fortune out of these ten kids, but unfortunately you're a Palestinian, no social security and no child allowance.'

Our laughter and screams were compounded by those of the workers from the village of Farkheh. They came running from the hill on the southern side. They were running towards us while screaming and looking back intermittently, Heeey . . .

Heeey . . . Heeey . . . Heeey . . . Ssssssss . . . Seeeee . . .
Whistle . . . Whistle . . . *Boker tov* . . . *Boker tov* . . . Hebrew
for good morning.

Some were cursing, some were nervously laughing and
others were making fun of the soldiers by whistling, but all
were running away from the soldiers who were standing a
kilometre or so to the southern side of our hill.

'We thought we could overcome them by walking along
the ridge of this hill and eventually sliding down the high
boulders, but *al-'arsat*, the fuckers took us by surprise. They
were hiding in the bushes. After most of us passed them,
they jumped, formed a cordon and trapped nearly everyone.
They beat the shit out of those in front. I saw two workers
jump over the cliff . . . God knows what they broke, probably a leg or an arm. But those of us a bit behind managed
to escape.'

I listened to a young boy give this breathless account. He
bent down, swirled around and lay flat on his back, his two
arms wide open as if crucified.

I stood up from under the olive tree and asked Mohammad
if he wanted to go and have a look. We walked south, in the
direction of the soldiers, and stopped in a safe spot where we
had a good view. In the very far distance we could see the
helmets of four soldiers guarding the arrested workers. Soon
Mohammad and I turned around and sneaked back to our
safer waiting spot.

Wait . . . wait . . . wait.

'*Ya zalameh*, let's just call it a day and go home. There
seems to be absolutely no chance today,' said one of the many
exasperated workers.

'What home? I'd rather die here than go back empty-handed,' replied his friend.

'Anyway, what would we do if we went back home now?'

'Die of boredom.'

'I'd rather die from a bullet than go back and sit on a stool in Ibrahim's coffee shop.'

'Poor Mazen.' Mohammad remembered his unemployed brother who sat in that coffee shop all day long. Mohammad sighed and added, 'What a life!'

'It's a dog's life.'

'You know that coffee shop would close if it wasn't for us.'

'Ibrahim, the owner of the coffee shop, waits anxiously for us every Friday evening. He would go bankrupt without us there.'

'We're the only customers who pay for their teas and coffees, otherwise it's all on credit.'

'Write down three coffees, Ibrahim . . . write down two teas, Ibrahim . . . write down one *narjeeleh* (hubbly bubbly pipe), Ibrahim . . . We promise to pay once we get a job . . . and you know most of us haven't worked for months on end.'

'What can he do? Most of the village men are unemployed and can't always pay.'

'Last night, after the football match, he announced he was going to close the coffee shop. He said, "It's losing business. I seem to be the village's caffeine pusher. Thank God, no free hashish."'

'Fuck, what are we waiting for? The soldiers won't go for some time and even if they did no one would give us a job this late in the day,' said one worker.

'I don't know about you guys, but I'm quitting for the day. It's already six-thirty and with the terrible luck we're having today we won't be there in five hours. *As-salamo 'alaikum*, I'm leaving.' He took a few steps but still hung around, not going far.

'Not over my dead body. I'll wait until the last day of my life,' I heard Saed say. He was standing next to the fire which was burning nicely now and had attracted a crowd around it.

'I'm leaving, goodbye.'

'Where to?'

'Home, where else?'

'My wife can't stand it when I go back empty-handed.'

'Do I have any other choice?'

'Yes, be patient and wait.'

'Wait for what?'

'Wait for the bloody soldiers to leave.'

'They won't.'

'Yes, they'll leave eventually.'

'Listen, guys, why don't we go on a demonstration towards the checkpoint? They won't arrest us all.'

'Yes, sure, they won't arrest us, they'll only shoot us all.'

'No they won't.'

'No one will hear about your demonstration except the angels,' said Mohammad.

'Okay, why don't we all run down at the same time? They can't arrest all of us. In this way some will pay the price by being arrested, while the rest will make it.'

'Look at us all, like sitting ducks.'

9.

Renewed Hope

Sunday May 13, 2007 [7:10 AM]
From Izzawiyyeh Village to
the Shade of the Olive Trees

It was a bit after seven in the morning when two young boys, aged ten or eleven, showed up. Each carried a huge metal coffee flask, almost as big as the boys themselves. Their appearance made me believe that that was it for the day. Each went in a different direction: around and around, around and around, selling their coffee to the many clusters of workers still hanging around, sitting under olive trees and holding on to the hope of a change in luck. In no time, the circles of workers were surrounded by many white plastic circles of coffee cups.

'Would you care for a cup of coffee?' asked Saed. Not wanting to refuse, I made the terrible mistake of drinking it. Before it even touched my stomach, I was in desperate need of the toilet. Having lost my pre-action anxiety, I had totally forgotten that not long ago I had had the runs. As discreetly as possible under the circumstances, I asked Mohammad to kindly accompany me back to Izzawiyyeh Village. At that point I had no other option.

'You've given up for the day.'

'Have you decided to go back?'

'If (President) Abu Mazen and (Prime Minister) Haniyyeh accompanied us for only one night, they might stop fighting one another.'

Not wanting to be among the first to 'give up', though a bit embarrassed, I had to explain,

'No . . . no . . . no, we just need to reach Izzawiyyeh, we'll be back soon.'

Understanding the nature of the need, there were no more questions.

It was the first time since we'd started in the morning that Mohammad couldn't keep up with me. At first I walked fast, then I loped, then rushed, then dashed, then sprinted, and in less than twenty minutes I was jogging in the middle of Izzawiyyeh's empty, dirty alleys. There was no one to talk to. I was truly getting desperate, and just when I was about to knock at someone's door, I heard Mohammad say, 'Good morning *Hajj*.'

I turned around and saw an old man in the front yard of his house. He had rested his frail body against a rubble wall, and with great difficulty he was planting a couple of olive seedlings. I walked towards Mohammad, greeting him.

'*Marhaba Hajj.*'

We got no reply.

'Hello there,' I yelled at the top of my lungs, but still no response.

'Probably deaf,' said Mohammad.

'That I can see . . . I'm not blind.'

We were literally on top of his tiny bent body and still it wasn't until Mohammad touched his shoulders that the *Hajj* realised someone was there.

'Good morning,' he screamed, thinking we were deaf.

'My mother is in bad need of a toilet, can she use yours?'

'Where are you from?' asked the old man.

Oh my God . . . if a typical endless Palestinian inquiry started, then I would be in deep . . .

'Are you visiting someone here?' the old man enquired.

'No, *Hajj*, we're on our way to work in Israel,' replied Mohammad.

'What about your mother?'

'My mother *desperately* needs a bathroom, *Hajj*.' Mohammad was losing his temper and I was giving up.

'Yes, but why are you taking your mother with you to Israel? I don't understand.'

'*Hajj*, I promise to explain *all*, but first can you show my mother where the toilet is?'

'Show your mother what?' asked the old man at the top of his voice.

'The TOILEEEEET,' Mohammad shouted, and a whole village woke up.

'Okay.' He finally got it. I slowly and desperately followed his small and shaky steps to an outhouse; I tell you, old people can be a nuisance sometimes. Once I recovered my composure, I stepped back into the garden where Mohammad and the deaf man were sitting. I joined in by pulling a third plastic chair next to Mohammad's. From the context of his talk, I could tell that the *Hajj* was speaking of the time of the British Mandate. Believe me, we had so many 'bad times' in our recent history that it wasn't always easy to guess.

'They took the poor man to the fields, tied him around the trunk of an olive tree and shot him at point-blank range.' This was all I needed during my 'no more coffee' break.

'This was a lesson meant for all. This was the fate of anyone who supported the partisans of the 1936 Revolt. It was the damn *Ingleez* that caused all of this mess. They brought the *Yahood* to settle in Palestine, and look what they do to us now: squeeze us and imprison us in our own land. My father told me that during the Ottoman days, Sultan Abdul Hamid II knew better. He didn't allow . . .'

Thank God Mohammad's mobile rang before the *Hajj* ventured into nineteenth-century Ottoman Palestine.

'WHAT? Really? Okay . . . Okay . . . we're coming right away.' Mohammad swiftly jumped out of his chair, which fell down behind him.

'Have they managed to cross?' I asked excitedly.

'Yep . . . Saed says we must come back at once. The jeep has just left, and all the workers have managed to cross.'

'Wow . . . let's try our luck then,' I said in a rather exhausted voice.

Tumbling down the same path for the third time in less than four hours, I wondered if perhaps Mohammad and I should've called it a day an hour earlier. Mohammad was happily jumping in front of me like a goat while I tiredly stumbled behind him.

Walk . . . walk . . . walk . . . jump, walk, jump . . . walk . . . walk . . . walk . . . stumble.

Bless their souls, both Abu Yousef and Comrade Muneer had been waiting for us. See how old people and communists weren't that bad after all? I looked across the highway and it was true, the blue neon light had vanished.

'Where is Murad?' Mohammad and I asked at exactly the same time.

'The minute the military jeep drove away, whizz, he rushed down this hill, up the opposite hill, and vanished,' explained Abu Yousef.

I must admit that the absence of Murad truly worried me. I realised it was Murad rather than Mohammad who had so far been my security blanket on this trip. Abu Yousef must've realised it as well.

'Don't worry, Suad . . . soon we'll catch up with him. The smaller the group the quieter and hence safer,' he reassured me.

Poor Murad, he must have been burdened by my obtrusive presence. He must have taken an even greater risk by running away from us.

'Let's hope this isn't a trap. Once, Murad and I managed to go around the hill and the soldiers pretended not to see us. As we succeeded in passing, all the other workers came running down the hill following our detour. That was exactly when the army arrested them . . . So let's hope it's not another one of the army's tricks,' said Abu Yousef.

I was so tired and fed up by now, I was hoping it was. Mohammad's mobile rang once more.

'Saed says all is clear. Hurry . . . we must run up the hill quickly.'

'Once we cross the highway, walk straight ahead and then up that hill again. Avoid going west towards the military camp. We're told there are still a few soldiers there.'

Like three gazelles and one cow, we went down the hill. I was sliding while resting my hand on Mohammad's left shoulder . . . run . . . run . . . run . . . breathe . . . breathe . . . breathe . . . up the metal band, across the high-way, up the middle concrete wall separating the two sides

88

of the highway, look right, wait for cars to pass, run across the highway once more . . . up the heavy metal railing on the other side of the highway and dash towards the steep slopes. Mohammad's shoulders were functioning as my heavyweight brakes.

The four of us kept running up the hill. But the distance between the two of us and the two of them, Abu Yousef and Muneer, was increasing, and soon Mohammad and I were left behind. At first we continued running fast up the hill . . . then walked fast . . . then walked . . . then walked slowly . . . then hardly walked at all . . . and then I took a mouthful of air, gasped, and stopped. I used my last drop of energy to look up the few hundred-metres-high hill where, in no time at all, the goat-like workers were vanishing over the summit. Mohammad was stuck alone with his breathless and fatigued boss.

'Can't take it anymore. I think I should give up, otherwise I will have a heart attack for sure.'

'God forbid, Suad,' said Mohammad with great concern. The look on his face made me believe that I had already had one.

My words were lost in the midst of my heartbeats and heavy breathing. Although I was about to drop dead, at least I had the wisdom to decide that having no story was much better than having no storyteller. I had tears in my eyes. I couldn't tell whether I was mourning the author or the impossible topic I had chosen for this book. I truly had no choice but to give up. I sat on a rock, spread out my two legs and tried to take a deep breath. I gathered enough energy for one sentence:

'Mohammad, why don't you call them and tell them I've collapsed, I've given up. Tell them not to wait for us.' Not that they had waited. I took a deeper breath and added, 'What a shame.'

'It's all right, Suad, we'll do it some other time.'

'What other time?' I simply couldn't think of another time, another day or even another life. I held my head between my hands and kept quiet. Mohammad did the same. He must have been missing the thrill of it all. I looked all around and there were hardly any workers in sight. I sat there and wondered to myself: would I have given up if I *truly* needed a job? I shed tears for Murad and friends.

'Never mind, Suad, you'll go on a diet, exercise for a month or two, and then we'll give it another try,' Mohammad tried to cheer me up.

'A month, that's a real compliment, my dear Mohammad. By the time I'm fit, and with the frantic speed with which the bloody Israelis are going about building this apartheid Wall, neither I nor anyone else will be able to make this trip walking or running.'

'No need for exercise then,' Mohammad giggled. We sat there for some time.

Much later, Mohammad's mobile rang.

'What, all arrested!! And where are you now? Okay . . . Okay . . . we'll wait for you here, we're almost on top of the hill,' I heard Mohammad say, as his face beamed.

'They all got arrested and you're smiling?' I asked inquisitively.

'Not all, most.'

'Who was that?'

'Muneer.'

'Was Murad arrested as well?'

'Murad! Never,' Mohammad said assertively and proudly.

'Where is he then?' I asked.

'They're coming back. Muneer tells us to hide under the large olive trees on top of the hill.'

'All right, under the large olive trees on top of hill . . . let's go.' I stood up with renewed hope of continuing the trip, fully energised. Once again, I started going up the hill, but effortlessly this time. Wow, what a bit of hope can do to us all.

As instructed, we reached the top of the hill and settled under the first huge olive tree we got to. Close by, and on the same hilltop, I could see many other groups of workers settling under other olive trees. I also spotted the man with a limp.

'See, not everyone was arrested,' I commented. *Offaa*! How Palestinians liked to exaggerate their sufferings. In a while, Mohammad stood up and waved his hand for Murad and company. From a distance I could see the three musketeers, sadly not four. They spotted Mohammad and came towards us. There was Muneer, followed by Saed and then Murad. For the first time ever I saw Murad dragging his feet behind them all. All the rest were missing, including my favourite companion, Abu Yousef.

'Fuckers, *al-'arsat,* they were hiding, waiting for us on the other side of the hill.' Our entire group has been arrested except for the three of us. You were lucky too,' explained Muneer.

'Where is Abu Yousef?' I enquired, though I knew.

'He should've waited. I told him to hold on for a bit, but he ran and ran and ultimately fell into the trap.'

So there are benefits to chubbiness and out-of-shape-ness, I thought to myself.

'Who else was arrested?' I asked, and started reciting their names one by one:

'Abu Yousef, Ramzi, young Mahmoud, Saed, the one in orange, and the guy with the thick silver necklace . . .'

'The one in orange is my brother, Musheer, and the one in the necklace is my other brother, Shaheer,' said Muneer.

'Oh, I see. The 'eers', I'd forgotten that they were your brothers.' I was rather embarrassed, but Muneer didn't seem too concerned.

He simply carried on: 'I saw them arrest Musheer, but I have a feeling that Shaheer may've made it with the first group. It was Abu Yousef who got arrested and that's why I came running back.'

'Good,' I found myself saying. Good for what, I didn't know. I guess for them not being arrested and for me having renewed hope to accompany them to work.

Muneer carried on: 'Poor Abu Yousef, he'll kill himself. He gets so mad, so mad when he gets arrested. Especially with Ramzi, who'll carry on making fun of him even while they're detained. Poor thing, he was arrested just the other day. One soldier got hold of him and beat the shit out of him, and when Abu Yousef objected by telling the soldier, "Shame on you, I'm your father's age," the soldier kept rubbing him in the dirt (*ma'masouh*).'

There was a little pause before Muneer carried on: 'The one thing that *really* gets me when I'm arrested is other work-ers' comments. *Ya zalameh*, man, instead of sympathising with you, they start lecturing you: how come you got arrested? Didn't you see the soldiers in front of your own eyes? Next time be alert, keep your eyes wide open, be awake.' Muneer stopped, then continued, 'There's nothing worse than getting arrested when you're almost there.'

'Are we almost there?' I asked optimistically, totally forgetting about Abu Yousef and the rest. It hadn't taken long for me to acquire the worker's resilience.

'No . . . We're still a long . . . long way. We're hardly halfway, that's if we ever make it today. It's already after nine and we won't make it to Segula before three or four.'

'Three or four!' I repeated, terrified.

'You know, it was never this bad; it was only a month ago that we could walk with hundreds of other workers at three in the morning. We would talk and laugh and no one would bother us. It has got worse with the new political developments and negotiations.'

I wanted to ask Muneer which political developments? What negotiations?

Since I didn't think there had been either, I kept quiet. Muneer carried on with typical Palestinian self-confidence, especially when analysing what Israel had done, was doing, or was about to do. Being a Palestinian and a communist, Muneer was doubly confident. I wondered how much more we would've lost if we hadn't had such astute political skills.

'You know, the Israelis don't want any international mediation or Middle Eastern interference . . .'

His astute political remark was interrupted by that of Mohammad: 'Negotiations are nonsense. They're only concessions from our side: concessions and more concessions, and what do we get in return? Nothing. We recognise them, they don't recognise us. We buy their products, they dump our products. Look at Gaza: poor farmers, they plant roses and flowers, and on Valentine's Day camels and sheep eat their products.'

I liked Mohammad's hardline position. But I didn't trust it much because he, like most Palestinians, kept shifting his position by the day.

'*Ya zalameh*, man, let them concede, what use is it all? Let them concede and just give us the right to move: to come and go just as the *Yahood* do. We don't want anything but to work and feed our children. What have we gained from the second intifada in 2000? We destroyed ourselves with our stupid slogan '*al-Aqsa wal-Aqsa*' (referring to the Aqsa Mosque). Is Jerusalem only ours? Let them have it, let them take it all. Look at the 1948 Arabs, they sold it and they built it[*]. Look at them today, they have a good life, a life even better than the Jews. They have everything: houses, money, jobs, fun, caaars, womeeen . . .'

'Yes, caaars and womeeen,' I heard Muneer say at exactly the same time as Saed and in the same emphatic tone.

'They can go wherever they wish. What more does anyone want from life?' Saed continued.

'Let's call someone to find out what's going on.' I had no clue as to why Mohammad interrupted the conversation at that very moment, though I knew well that he had a fetish for both cars and women. Had I not decided I wasn't a woman on this trip, I would've put an end to all their sexist remarks, but I must admit I was enjoying the Big Boys' political analysis. 'I am not calling anyone anymore, I must have spent at least twenty shekels this morning just calling this and calling that. I swear to God, between the cigarettes and the phone, I must've spent at least fifty shekels so far, not counting transport. It will be a day's pay before we even get to work. Man,

[*] The Palestinians who stayed in Palestine after the 1948 war and the creation of the state of Israel.

fuck Jawwal (the Palestinian telephone company), Cellcom (the Israeli company) is much cheaper. The other day I called Amman for three minutes twenty-four seconds and it cost fifteen shekels, forty-six agoras.' Since I'd never met a comrade with accurate calculations, I was impressed with Muneer's.

'Let us just sit back and pray that we're not surrounded by soldiers on all sides,' said Mohammad.

'Look, look down there, near the sewage, there are a bunch of workers led by two soldiers. It seems some workers were arrested even before they made it up the hill.'

Lucky them, I almost said.

'Some before the hill, some after the hill, and I have a feeling we're sandwiched in-between,' Mohammad continued with his heart-stopping comments.

I turned my head to the side and looked at Murad. Silently he sat aside, not that he'd been talkative all along, but still, not a single word, not a comment, not even a sigh in this last grave episode. In spite of his physical proximity, Murad was apart; he was absent; in reality, he wasn't there at all. While he gazed at the very far horizon, I gazed at his challenged, fox-like face. His thick black connected eyebrows framed his big, fuming hazelnut eyes. The downward tilted head, supported by a rough worker's fist, overstressed his frustrated look. His contracted facial muscles and his stiff, slightly parted lips made me take in how angry he must've been.

Where was he?

What was he thinking of? Soon I was lost in his world, which seemed to be slowly slipping away from between his strong firm fingers.

95

Was he missing Lily? Or was he missing the potential employer who made it possible for him to pamper her? For him to be 'Murad the lover,' sweet and attentive.

Was he simply missing the virtual women with bikinis stuck on the wall of that tiny room? Or was he missing some other non-kosher women that Mohammad had whispered in my ears about? Was he missing his life as 'Murad the fun guy', buying big bottles of beer and packets of cigarettes and enjoying the risky and rough seas of both Jaffa and Tel Aviv?

He couldn't have been missing the eerie unfinished concrete structure where he had been sleeping lately.

He couldn't have been missing the many 'dogs' that barked at him, or the employer who robbed him of a day's or a week's pay by reporting him to the police. I wondered what scared Murad more, being arrested by the Israeli army or the vicious border police, as he ventured west, or going back east in the direction of the unemployed coffee shop in his own village? The uncharacteristic look of desperation on Murad's face swelled the anxiety within me. At that very moment I realised how much I wanted him to utter one word or his usual 'this way' phrase. Oh, how much I was in need of that promising optimistic face and that comforting, subtle smile of his.

To reassure myself that this was just a momentarily angry and frustrated Murad, I recalled his delightful photo album and my favourite facet of Murad and his life(s): I thought of the beaming face of joyful and hopeful boyish Murad as he posed in a studio, passionately holding a Spanish guitar. Standing under a palm tree, a rose-coloured sea as the backdrop. 'My dream *was* to become a musician and wander around freely.'

'Why *was*? Why in the past? Remember, you're only twenty-one.' Surprised, I answered him back. Only now I understood that it was the 'wandering around freely' that enchanted Murad rather than the Spanish guitar which he held closely to his then-dainty body. Only now I understood how unattainable that little dream of moving freely seemed in a hard-hitting life, a big part of which was spent between chunks of concrete stumbling blocks. It was his ancestors' ancient olive trees that now offered him the shade under which he, and others, patiently waited. But now that he was deprived of being 'Murad the diligent and conscientious worker', I saw a determined face: 'Murad the defiant'; 'Murad the fighter'; though his Second World War rifle, for the right reasons, was missing.

What scared him most was to be trapped in the no work option in his own country. And what scared *me* most was the hopelessness and the helplessness I saw in the photograph of bearded 'Murad the pious'. That incredibly serious expression, posing in front of an infinite path that some believed would lead to heaven.

Or perhaps to yet another hell.

As I closed my eyes, trying to freely wander around, listening to Murad's dream, I recalled what Mohammad once told me: 'Since he was a kid, playing in the streets with other youngsters, Murad couldn't stand losing. He is relentless, he is unyielding, never defeated, and he'll keep at it until he gets it . . . Murad never gives up.'

'Why don't I go around and ask other workers if they know what's going on?' Saed's suggestion brought Murad and me back to reality.

'The blind leading the blind, why would they know any better?'

'I'll go ask, I'm fed up waiting.'

'Go, but keep your head down. Don't let the soldiers spot you.'

There was a long silence and a bit of tension. In order to lighten the mood I initiated a conversation.

'So, do they normally shoot at you?'

'Not really . . . they mostly shoot in the air as they did this morning . . . But some workers fall down while running away, and end up breaking a leg or an arm, that's all.'

No breaking of any legs or arms so far. *Brava* Suad.

We simply sat there and waited.

10.

Nothing Makes Sense, Why Should I?

Sunday May 14, 2007 [10:20 AM]
From 'Azzoun to Banksy's* Wall

'Hurry up . . . hurry up . . . they took them away. We can go, come on, get up,' someone yelled from a distance. In a split second they all ran away and dissolved. Once more I found myself alone with Mohammad.

'Wait . . . wait, Mohammad, I don't quite get it.'

'Let's go, Suad, this is our last chance to make it with Murad and friends.'

'But where is my hat? Can't go without it.'

'Here it is, let's go.'

I grabbed my hat and tape recorder and went . . . run, run, run . . . run, run, run, run . . . run . . . run . . . run . . . run . . . run, run . . . run . . . run . . . run, stop, take a long breath and continue running.

Breathe . . . breathe . . . and a deeper breath. I wasn't going to lose my energy and breath this time.

Run . . . run . . . run . . . run.

★   ★   ★

* Robert Banks (Banksy), a well known British graffiti artist whose nine provocative stencilled murals on the Wall became internationally famous.

'Where is Murad?'

'Don't know.'

'And the other two?'

'Don't know *Suad,* just keep running.' It was the first
time that I got the feeling that even Mohammad was getting
fed up with me. What would happen if Mohammad decided
to leave me and go? In my heart I knew he wouldn't. I
looked up and once more I spotted the old man with the
limp. With my eyes fixed on him, I kept running. Each time
I looked at him I was energised. I ran . . . I ran fast . . . I
ran even faster. My heart was pumping hard . . . at least the
terrain was flat.

'Where are we now?'

'We're close to 'Azzoun,' I heard someone say.

Good, so we're not alone.

'Suad, run a bit faster, here are Saed and Muneer waiting
for us. I can see them, let's go.'

True, I also could see Saed and Muneer waiting for us just
before a highway.

'Where's Murad?'

'He dissolved like salt.'

'So what now?'

'Ten minutes and we get to 'Azzoun.'

'But I thought 'Azzoun was surrounded by a fence, I mean
a wall on all sides.'

'Yes, it is.'

Nothing made sense so I kept my breath and concentrated on
my stride. Mohammad's mobile rang. It was Fadia from our
office, Riwaq.

'Fadia says she ran out of paper and wants me to buy her

some,' said Mohammad, giggling. I also burst out laughing. I had totally forgotten that other worlds existed in my life.

'Tell her you're busy.'

'They're wondering where we are.'

'Tell them to fuck off, tell them we're in the lowest point on earth: Jericho.'

Once again Mohammad made sure to keep me entertained, 'You see that house over there?' He pointed to a small concrete structure in the distance.

'What about it?'

'*Once*, a collaborator from the village of Sanniria used to hide in it and shoot at workers. He injured many and killed a few.'

'A Palestinian collaborator from the village of Sanniria, shooting at workers!' I repeated it so as to grasp why a Palestinian would shoot at his fellow Palestinians. I paused, then asked, 'And when was *once?*'

'First intifada,' Mohammad replied.

'You mean in 1987. Twenty-some years ago?'

I guess Mohammad was trying to boast about his glorious past. Since he was only six years old then, I said nothing and simply concentrated on my pace.

We soon caught up with Muneer and Saed. Murad was still ahead.

'We're almost in 'Azzoun. Do you see the soldiers over there?' explained Muneer.

'Soldiers?' I panicked.

'No, no, don't worry, these soldiers won't shoot at us or arrest us,' he reassured me.

'Why not?' I asked.

'These soldiers don't arrest workers. They just make sure that no one from 'Azzoun leaves the village, and don't ask me why not, but they won't stop us from going into 'Azzoun.'

No need to understand; just follow. I was talking to myself. Okay, I would surrender to the lack of logic.

'Be careful while crossing the road,' Mohammad alerted me.

'Wouldn't it be hilarious if we got run over by a car after all of this?'

I held Mohammad's hand tightly and crossed the first half of the road, then over the concrete barrier, then the other two lanes. I found myself just a few metres away from the 'non-arresting soldiers'. And indeed they were peacefully guarding the entry point into 'Azzoun, a small village with three thousand inhabitants.

'Stay close to me, don't let the soldiers see me,' I urged Mohammad and Muneer.

'Don't worry, they'll probably think you're a woman journalist,' commented Muneer.

'A journalist, perhaps, a woman, I doubt,' I mumbled to myself.

Muneer's comment reminded me of all the unnecessary effort I had made to look like one of the Big Boys. Nevertheless, I tucked my dangling hair under the cap, buttoned up my jacket, bent my head downwards and passed right by the four Israeli soldiers standing next to the gated entrance of 'Azzoun.

'One of the soldiers is staring at you,' Mohammad murmured.

'Just ignore him and don't look at him,' I whispered back as I hurriedly walked away.

Up and down a few dirt mounds, and a hundred metres or so, and once again I was in the company of hundreds of workers. Most were sitting around, having a midday coffee break from the hard work they had (or hadn't) done so far. On one of the two concrete steps in front of a small shop, I spotted the boy-in-red.

'Hey . . . how are you, my friend? So you haven't been arrested . . . that's good,' I greeted him.

'I got arrested but ran away. They arrested many workers from our village but I decided to run away,' he repeated proudly.

'Weren't you afraid? Isn't it risky to run away? They could've shot at you,'

I warned him a bit too late.

'Well, I wanted to look for my mobile phone. It fell on the ground. It cost five hundred shekels and I wasn't going to leave it for them.' Again, I didn't quite get the logic or sequence of things, but never mind.

Meanwhile, Mohammad went into the shop and got us some water and a few bars of my childhood addiction, KitKat. I sat next to the boy-in-red and started chatting with other workers around me. Before long we were treated to more show-off time, but sadly with no Ramzi this time.

'What suffering! It's good exercise; five to six hours of walking and you'll be in shape for the Olympics in China. Look at us,' one pointed at his skinny body.

I felt as if they had all been watching my heavy weight as I stumbled along breathlessly. Come to think of it, except for communist Muneer and I, all of them were stick thin. The same worker carried on, 'This way we also get to know the geography of our country.'

★   ★   ★

If anything, this trip had confused the hell out of me. I had no idea where we had been, where we were, or where we were heading. The more I thought about it the more I began to worry about my readers: how was I to remember all of this and how was I to explain things for them? If it wasn't clear to me, then how would my readers understand? Anyway, why should my readers understand something I couldn't grasp?

'Mohammad . . . come on, we need to get going,' yelled Saed from a distance.

'What, now?' I jumped from my step and followed Saed.

'We need to find a Ford to take us to the 'Azzoun wall,' Saed said.

'Don't go now, the soldiers just arrested a few workers next to the electricity station,' I heard someone say from a distance.

'Come on guys, let's go,' Saed yelled nervously.

The five of us got onto the bus, one after another. We were soon joined by workers from other villages. I sat next to Mohammad in the front seat. The bus was so noisy I could hardly follow any of the conversations around me. The only thing I could hear was the clutter of the bus engine: click . . . click . . . click . . . click. For the first few kilometres, the bus went along a semi-asphalted road, but soon it turned onto a narrow dirt road. Someone was yelling from the back seat, in an attempt to tell the driver what to do and where to go.

'Don't worry: I'm from here, I live here, I work here, and I know exactly where the big hole in the fence is. I'll take you to a place where you can get through the fence; no cameras, no shooting, and no electric fence.'

I began to hallucinate about the non-electrified part of the barbed wire of the fence, and before I knew it, we were face to face with an Israeli military jeep. It was on the same narrow dirt path but coming in the opposite direction. If neither had stopped we would have had a head-on collision. I don't know what got hold of me but I was foolishly laughing and singing out loud,

'*Ya habibi . . . Ya habibi . . . Akalna hawa . . . Akalna hawa . . . Ya habibi*. Oh my love . . . Oh my love . . . Oh my love . . . We're done with . . . we're done with . . . My beloved. Our love affair is over.'

The driver simply slowed down and pulled over to the side. There was complete silence in the bus. There was an air of apprehension about our final surrender. So it was the 'arrest option' that we were ultimately fated for. Except for the bus rattle, there was total silence. And even that soon stopped as the driver turned off his engine.

'Let's see what their reaction will be to a woman worker,' being an egomaniac, I whispered to Mohammad. I don't know why, but I was sort of amused rather than scared. Somehow, I found it easier to confront a soldier than to trust him with my back. But to our utter surprise the military jeep simply passed us and kept on going.

We turned our heads to the left, then behind, following the armoured vehicle as it disappeared. I wondered what kind of soldiers these were. Not the 'shoot at us', not the 'arrest us', not the 'beat us up', and not the 'Azzoun 'non-arresting guards'. They must have been the 'pretend not to see' soldiers.

'What the hell is going on? Didn't they see us? Didn't they realise we're workers on the run?'

'Of course they did; they decide what they want, whenever they want. That's the real power,' Muneer remarked.

'*Al-'arsat* . . . Fuckers . . . '*arsat* . . . fuckers,' I kept saying to myself (and to Mohammad).

Bizarre! Some saw us from afar, and others shot at us. Some ran after us, and others trapped us. Some arrested us, and others beat us up. Some let us through a guarded gate, and others turned a blind eye.

And you wonder why the Palestinians are totally confused and fucked up!

The unrelenting rattle of the bus was finally getting to me. At that very moment I truly wanted some serenity to figure out the lack of logic of it all.

I found myself right in front of the Wall.

I looked at it and froze and for the first time on this trip real fear got hold of me: my legs were weakening, my feet were going numb, while my body stiffened . . .

'Come on, Suad, let's get going. This is *very* critical and dangerous. Here you've got to run as fast as you can, here is where they really shoot at us, here is where we cross from the West Bank to Israel,' Muneer explained.

'Did you say from the West Bank to Israel?' I asked out loud. 'Muneer, do you mean to tell me that we've been on "our side" all this time? And what have we been doing for the last ten fucking hours? And why have they been shooting at us, running after us, beating us up and arresting us if we are still on "our side", on our land, on the West Bank side? If the Wall separates Palestine from Israel then why are they harassing us on our side?'

'Come on, Suad, if we succeed in crossing this bit of the wall, we'll be safe, no one will harass us anymore and we can finally get to work . . .' Muneer reassured me.

So we're *not* harassed when in Israel, but we're harassed when in Palestine; we're safe in Israel, but not safe in Palestine. Soon I was talking to myself, and for the first time ever I knew why mad people talk to themselves.

Nothing made sense, why should I?

11.

Animals' Nightmare

Children's Fable
Timeless, Space-less

I looked left and I looked right. At one end of the Wall, I could see the glittering lights of the city of London. At the other, some seven hundred kilometres away, I could see the dim lights of Zurich. I pulled my neck and head back and looked up at the eight-metre-high concrete Wall with great difficulty. I could see the tops of Berlin's buildings. I saw tens of workers, I saw hundreds of workers, I saw thousands of workers. They all ran towards that Wall.

Some were at the bottom of it, some were on top of it, and some were stuck in between.

Some whizzed through it, some bounced off it, and some had their limbs stuck to it.

Some were falling on 'our side', some were falling on 'their side', and others were stuck on No Man's Wall.

In the midst of it all, I looked for the man with the limp, but failed to spot him.

I ran out of energy and despaired.

I saw myself shot dead against that Wall.

I stood there and cried.

★   ★   ★

I cried so much my soul hurt.

I stood there and cried.
  Like a baby I cried.
  Like a child I cried.
  Like the day when my first beloved dog died, I cried.

I watched the dark and elongated shadows of my childhood animals bounce off that wall. My late mother's soft voice was echoing in my ears: *Susti habibti, there is nothing to be afraid of, animals are not ghosts and they hurt no one . . .* There was a long pause before she added, *unless we hurt them. Come, habibti, come closer, give me your hand, see . . .* One thing my mum forgot to do was to cut that umbilical cord between animals and myself.

And there they were next to that monstrous Wall. I could see them, one . . . by . . . one: Reem, my beloved Arabian gazelle who taught me how to sprint like a bullet on the slippery terrace of our house in Amman as we ran after one another. There he was, bashing his head, trying to run across that Wall. One of his long curved horns was missing. He swirled and swirled until his shadow hit mine. Totally dazed, we stared at one another: tears mixed with black kohl ran down our cheeks. We hugged and cried.

'Where is our dear Sukkar?' I asked after his blind wife.

'I went to search for food to feed her and our little ones, but when I came back I found this madness.' My concerned look for blind Sukkar and her little ones made him burst out in tears.

'What about the other members of our animal farm?' I asked anxiously.

'Shee ... just follow me,' he whispered, and turned around. Like a toddler, I ran quickly after him; I held tightly to his remaining horn, which wobbled.

Mickey, my adorable dog who, for twelve years, day in, day out, accompanied me to school, was swirling in the air like a cyclone. Sambo, my black cat who licked my tears whenever I shed them. And I tell you she worked hard; there she was, speedily flying down with her four legs apart.

As far as my childhood memory went, Sasha the monkey was always Mum's favourite. Sasha was aimlessly swinging up and down on both sides of that Wall. She had always been good at monkey business. Sasha, that is, not my mum. In the distance was Basalt, my patient, nine-hundred-year-old turtle. When I was a child, Basalt told me Crusader fables that started but never ended:

'We carried coded letters back and forth for the partisans in our shells ... and that was how we overcame their two hundred years of bloody occupation.'

I watched while, on a mound next to the Wall, Basalt banged her shell against that Wall. She banged and banged until her shell cracked. I rushed towards her and looked closely at the mound where she had collapsed; it was made out of broken turtle shell. Secret numbers, letters and yellow butterflies were blowing everywhere in the wind.

1 ... 2 ... 3

A big group of our neighbour's pink pigs bashed their protruding noses against that Wall. 1 ... 2 ... 3 ... They banged so hard and for so long that their noses looked like TV satellite dishes and, as a result, they could communicate with the rest of their family members stuck behind that Wall.

Pigs.

New Grey Land.

My failing emotions carried me out of my childhood garden and neighbourhood and into today's New Grey Land, where lizards frantically changed their colours into shades of grey. When I marvelled at this, one explained, 'With so little green and so much concrete, it became much safer to camouflage ourselves in shades of grey.'

A bunch of moles with huge paws were hysterically digging holes in the asphalt road that ran parallel to the concrete Wall. Their bleeding paws left red traces on the black asphalt.

'Our underground earth tunnels have been blocked and destroyed. The earthworms, on which we once fed, have been removed, and tons and tons of asphalt and concrete have been poured in their place. A whole generation of baby moles has died. Look at us. We have all become cheap labourers in an emergency archaeological dig.'

When nothing made sense to me, and I looked absolutely flabbergasted, the chief mole of the expedition explained:

'Because of our environmentally sensitive digging skills and expertise, UNESCO and the World Monuments Fund commissioned us to document damages caused to archaeological sites along this Wall. Since the contractors were in such a hurry to build this Wall they messed up and destroyed layers and layers of cultures and civilizations.'

He took me by the hand and moaned, 'Look at the mess they left behind, look what we've got.'

In a big flat Canaanite ceramic pot I found a bunch of bronze and gold coins. One by one I carefully picked them up and read their index cards: 'Persian Satrap (399 BC), bronze Macedonian coins (336 BC), bronze drachmas, Phoenician mint, Palestinian mint, Herod the Great (37 BC) . . .'

I looked around and found shards of pottery everywhere.

'These we can put together: some shards are Greek, some are Roman, and some are Byzantine. The ones we can't do much about are the many layers of early and late Arab periods. These have been damaged beyond repair, in spite of fourteen centuries of existence,' the chief mole explained with a distressed expression on his face. 'This is what we archaeologists refer to as *irreversible damage*.' He hid his tears from my tears. I turned my head away.

A hedgehog hurried by and bragged, 'Fourteen centuries of Arab and Muslim rule in Palestine is *no time*; my ancestors have been on this earth for the last fifteen million years. But nevertheless, that is not the point: we cannot recall such recklessness in the environment.'

Okay, I may have had some respect for the hedgehog's positions on environmental issues, but somehow they always had a sort of unethical and wishy-washy position concerning Arab and Muslim time and stands concerning Israel. Hedgehogs also had this terrible habit of making a blunt statement and then rolling themselves into their spikes and hiding from it all. They are so introverted and so unreal. They were worse than lizards; lizards changed colour but hedgehogs became funny spiky balls. They were so deceptive too. The first time I saw one, I was a little girl. I was playing with the little boys of the neighbourhood. We found a bunch of round balls, and

112

wondered why they were so spiky, but that didn't stop us from playing a game of bowling for hours on end, until one got tired and unfolded itself. We got so scared that we ran away and trembled for hours.

I looked around and saw herds of sheep and goats feeding on mounds of big red carnations and roses. As I stood there in a daze one black goat came closer and clarified, 'We're helping Palestinian farmers get rid of their produce. Israel prevents them from exporting it to Europe, and since we don't like waste, we have changed into carnation-eaters.'

'Mmmm. Good for you and *buon appetito,*' I replied.

I found myself in a landscape of uprooted olive trees. Later, I learned that this happened to be one of the Seven Wonders of the World, as recorded in the *Guinness Book of Records*: the fastest uprooting of olive trees in the history of mankind. Over one and a half million olive trees uprooted in less than a *year.* On the ground I found a promotional brochure that read: 'Tourists of the world come and see with your own eyes how Israel made the desert bloom.' But since the world continues to be dangerously 'anti-Semitic' no one came to see.

I saw a woman in black, mourning an olive tree. She hugged its crooked trunk tightly and wept quietly. I saw a man reading a book entitled *Memoirs of an Olive Tree.* He wept like a child. Right next to the Wall sat a camel. His big droopy eyes and his voluptuous lips beamed when I looked at him,

'Be patient and do not despair. This is all temporary; it will soon disappear. The problem with you, mankind, is that you have a short memory, and hence never learn from history.'

113

He sat back and chewed on an olive branch.

In the Olive Trees Memorial Park I was stopped by a fox, an activist fox. He asked me to sign a petition addressed to Al Gore and cc'ed to God. The petition read:

We members of the 'Fauna and Flora of Palestine' before God call on Al Gore, and all nature lovers, to intervene on our behalf. By constructing this monster, mankind has violated all International Environmental Conventions and caused unprecedented damage:

Destroyed our natural habitats
Blocked our natural paths above and below ground
Demolished our nesting places in trees, caves and sub-terrains
Separated us from our beloved ones on the other side of the Wall
Deprived us of our livelihood and our grazing grounds
Resulted in the extinction of a few rare species

We the undersigned have talked, prayed and begged God so many times. He once sent a secret message that read: 'I apologise for not being able to address this very sensitive issue. I can't do much about your sufferings in my Holy Land, at least not in this life-cycle but perhaps in another.' His sorrowful words made many of us despair and commit suicide.

I looked at the bottom and added my signature to a long, long list of signatories: foxes, chickens, gazelles, cats, dogs, hedgehogs, moles, tortoises, ants, wild pigs, puppies, wild orchids, horses, cows, bees, Spanish broom, wild sage, wild oregano, and an endless list of species. The list was too long to remember. However, one thing I did notice: there wasn't a single human signature on that list.

I added mine.

12.

Banksy's Wall: Time for Hope

The wall "essentially turns Palestine into the world's largest open prison."
Banksy

I was about to lose hope in mankind when
I heard soft whispers
I looked behind and saw little girls and boys right next to
    Banksy's Wall
I slowly regained hope.

I saw a little girl searching an Israeli soldier. His face was against an eight-metre high Wall, his hands up in surrender and his rifle on the ground right next to her. While she searched the lower part of his pants, she looked at me and smiled; her smile told me not to *ever* despair.

I saw a little girl flying up the Wall. She was dressed in a cute short skirt while her braid flew in the air. In one hand she clutched eight round black balloons, and in the other hand she clutched the limp-man. Though she was tiny, she effortlessly carried him across that Wall. I stood there and clapped enthusiastically for the flying balloon girl.

I heard a little boy whisper 'Come this way'. He came closer, took me by the hand and led me to Banksy's cosy living room. He made me sit on one of the two big, white upholstered armchairs. I sat there, took a deep breath, and all was fine.

I looked out of the window carved into that wall and saw an alpine landscape. I also saw workers running through two big holes cracked in the Wall; a little boy stood on the other side of the Wall whispering to the workers, 'Come this way . . . Come this way.'

I couldn't tell what language the boy was speaking. At first it sounded like Banksy's English accent, but when I listened carefully I realised it was Hebrew. And since most, if not all, workers understood and spoke Hebrew, they ran towards him. He leaned out of the big hole and helped them, one by one, to pass to the other side of the Wall.

From my comfortable living room I could see two little boys standing beneath another gap in the Wall. They were murmuring to more and more workers to come forward. One boy held a bucket, the other a spade, while tens, maybe hundreds of workers passed through the hole that opened onto the vista of a lush tropical paradise.

I kneeled out of the living room window and I looked further up. I saw a rope ladder that went to the top of the Wall. Yet another little boy sat under the snake-like ladder, offering his tiny hand to hundreds and hundreds of workers. Like olive-tree hikers, they went step by step up the painted rope ladder until they got to the top of the Wall. I could see their bodies twist as they climbed up to the other side of the Wall.

I saw a light brown horse peek his head out of a small framed window cut into the upper part of the concrete Wall. While his body disappeared behind the Wall, he gave instructions as to when it was safe to climb up.

'Now,' I heard him say. I saw the horse smiling whenever a worker made it safely across that Wall. I saw him dance for joy when the limping man flew. His thin legs could be seen from another low square window that Banksy had drawn on that Wall. Had it not been for my imagination and for the cosy living room of Banksy's canvas wall, I wouldn't have been able to gather the energy or the morale required to carry on with my trip. I placed the artist Robert Banks' (Banksy) book *Wall and Piece* on the little coffee table he had drawn on what he described as 'the ugliest and most intrusive wall' and carried on. Thanks, Banksy.

I looked back at the wall and went: Ctrl-Alt-Delete.

And all was fine.

13.

On the Other Side

Once the animals' nightmare and my daydreaming had come to an end

I ran and ran . . . I ran and ran . . . I ran and ran . . . until

I reached Mohammad and Comrade Muneer.

They had patiently waited there.

They both stretched their muscular arms as far as they could.

They widened . . . and widened the slit in the fence-wall until my fatigued body slipped through that Wall.

Yes, I made it through that Wall.

Wow . . . Thank you, Mohammad . . . Thank you, Muneer.

I was *finally* on the other side of the Wall.

14.

On Their Side

Back to civilization: the four-lane highways with their black and white demarcations; the wide pavements along which we dragged our tired, dusty and, in my case, swollen feet; the green roundabout; the many traffic lights; the little park next to the big-spanned bridge, all of this made me realise that we were in 'Israel proper', as opposed to where we had come from: 'Israel not so proper' . . . *and yet.*

From a distance, over the bridge, I spotted the limping man, his pace rising and falling on a levelled, smooth and tiled surface, in contrast to the natural rocky and terraced fields over which we had all shambled. His limp was much more apparent.

He was still going.

'Suad, see the bridge over there?' noted Muneer.

'Yes,' I replied as I looked away from the labourer over to the bridge itself.

'Right under it is where bus 185 to Petah Tikva stops.'

Under bridge . . . bus stop . . . bus number 185 . . . the Israeli town of Petah Tikva (which means 'Gateway of Hope' in Hebrew), I found myself repeating after Muneer.

'What about it?' I asked, perplexed.

'We'll try to get on it.'

'Try to get on the bus . . . mmm . . . I see.'

We were to try and get on a bus! We had been so much on the run that it felt rather bizarre to do such mundane things as get on a bus, and then it hit me: so we're to get on the bus with *them*.

'Are we getting on the same bus with them?' I asked out loud.

'Yes,' was Muneer's short straightforward reply.

It sounded so natural to all of them, even to Mohammad, that I gave it more serious thought. So far we had managed to speedily run away from them (in my case, breathlessly and not so elegantly) and now we were to be on the same bus with them. I was trying hard to understand the new rules of this part of the game. We ran away from the Israeli soldiers and now, so casually, we were to join the Israeli civilians. Was that it?

Dr. Jekyll and Mr. Hyde.

I was truly relieved to know that the so far not fatal fifteen-hour march was finally coming to an end and that I was *a terra*. I could hardly stay in a vertical position. The thought of sitting down on a seat, even a bus seat next to one of them, cheered me up.

'Wow, how wonderful it will be to finally sit down on a comfortable seat,' I said out loud. No one paid any attention or seemed to care. I couldn't help but feel nervous. I guess running away from *them* had been the mode, not only for the last fifteen hours, but for the last forty-some years.

As we walked through a small park in the direction of the promised bus my mind drifted off. It was going through the different scenes of the 2005 Golden Globe Award-winning film, *Paradise Now* by Hany Abu-Assad. My heart was beating as fast as Saeed's (Saeed actually is the male variant of my name Suad, meaning happy), one of the two heroes (I'd better say one of the two main characters, Saeed and Khaled)*. I vividly recalled the scene in which Saeed stood waiting for an Israeli bus which he planned to get on and detonate a belt of explosives wrapped around his chest. Just before Saeed gets on the bus he sees a little child getting on board and, as a result, he decides not to get on, but eventually he blows himself up on another bus.

I looked around in search of the little girl (in that film she stood next to her father at the bus stop), but neither she nor her father were there. I found myself nervously and suspiciously inspecting people around me. So far, all were friendly and familiar faces. There was sweet and naive Mohammad, tenacious and alert Murad and the wildly handsome Saed. I looked for sturdy Comrade Muneer but he was missing.

I turned around in search of Muneer. In no time I spotted him in the little park just behind the bus stop. He, like me, was acting a bit nervously. I watched as he dusted his beige pants, especially around his protruding and rounded buttocks. He then rolled his trousers up once, twice, three times until they reached an inch or two below his knees. Having neatly rolled his trousers up, he rapidly unbuttoned his dark blue shirt, took it off and swiftly shoved it in his huge rucksack.

* The Arabic name 'Saeed' is not related to the name 'Saed', although it may appear to be similar in English transliteration.

Wearing a white undershirt, Muneer pulled out a bright yellow T-shirt and put it on.

In the same animated way he took off his long-sleeved acrylic shirt. The sleeveless, thin cotton T-shirt accentuated every single muscle of his firm and well 'worked-out' body. He swiftly leaned against a small parapet, took off his crooked and dusty black moccasin shoes and slipped into the brown sandals typical of Israeli men (often made by Palestinians from Hebron). Finally, he zipped out funky-looking dark sunglasses, behind which his familiar eyes disappeared.

The minute I understood what was going on with Muneer I thanked God no other comrades were around to see what had become of their 'People's Party'. It seemed that as I was busy watching a virtual *Paradise Now* I was missing the real show: how to pass for an Israeli. Since Israelis were not exactly French or Italian when it came to fashion it didn't take much to look like one. But to act like one was a completely different story.

Murad must have smeared at least half a tube of hair gel into his already unconventional, ridiculous spiky hair. Since his light grey slacks were more like shorts below his knees, he didn't need to roll them up. He also had a body-tight sleeveless T-shirt. His sunglasses, which matched his hairstyle, had silver red frames and reflective mirror glass. The reflections of the lenses could easily, if not kill, at least cause sunstroke to anyone who might stare at him for more than thirty seconds. And that was exactly what I did. I eventually turned my head towards Saed.

Realising that it took much more to change his looks, and the unfair world in which he lived, Saed opted for simpler tricks: he rolled his short sleeves up to his armpit; straightened the collar of his orange shirt, covering his neck in a sleek manner; reversed his cap from front to back; and wrapped a black pouch around his waist to match the leather black strap around his wrist and the thick chain around his neck. Saed's last touch of camouflage was to tie his light brown wavy hair into a ponytail. Since his hair wasn't that long, only half was wrapped up and the rest was dangling.

The one thing I thought missing was a ring in one ear or even on his belly. He, unlike Muneer and Murad, looked truly cool. So cool he went beyond Israeli.

The exhaustion of the last fifteen hours didn't stop me from noticing how handsome Saed was. All along the trip, whenever I had a chance to steal a glance at him I did. I was trying to figure out who he looked like, and I finally made up my mind: he was a hybrid of Russell Crowe and Joaquin Phoenix in *Gladiator*. His figure resembled that of Crowe, and the slight harelip in his upper lip made him look like Phoenix. No wonder Lily loved him more than she loved tiny, skinny and rough-looking Murad.

But Saed almost spoiled it by wearing ridiculous-looking sunglasses. I don't know what it is about Palestinians; they all believe they can pass for an Israeli, regardless of how typically Arab they look, the second they put on sunglasses. Having figured it out, most Israeli soldiers asked Palestinians to take off their sunglasses (at least) as a 'security' measure at checkpoints.

All of a sudden I felt that the bus station was changing from a scene out of *Paradise Now* to a scene from the video clip *Chic Point: Fashion for Israeli checkpoints* by the Palestinian artist Sharif Waked. All was in place. Except for Mohammad and me, the three could pass for Israelis at least in appearance (thank God not in abrasiveness). Muneer, Murad and

124

Saed felt safer and more confident with their new looks. I watched them carefully and realised that the one reality they couldn't change was the poverty-stricken class to which they belonged.

But believe me they were trying very hard.

My heart skipped a beat when Muneer announced, 'Here it comes.' I looked to my left. Sure enough bus number 185 was indeed arriving. The slower the bus went, the faster my heart beat, until both stopped. Finally it (I mean the bus) pulled in. I could see the faces of the Israeli passengers on the bus one . . . by . . . one. There seemed to be dozens of apprehensive eyes looking down at us. Or was it my apprehension reflected in their eyes? My first reaction was to give up the ride and simply run away.

First in line was Comrade Muneer; second the gladiator Saed; then me, pretentious bourgeois; then the socially upwardly mobile Mohammad; and last, the working-class spiky Murad. As Muneer and Saed got on the bus I took a deep breath and followed. I was standing on the first step of the bus waiting for Muneer to finish his Hebrew conversation with the bus driver when I noticed Saed's left palm giving a sign to go back. I immediately stepped back, as did Mohammad and Murad.

'*Al-maniac*,' I heard Muneer say as he jumped off the bus.

'What is it?' I asked.

'He wanted to see my ID or my work permit.'

'And what did you tell him?' I asked.

'I told him I had forgotten my ID at home. The fucker said, "Then go get it".'

'The fucker,' I repeated.

Amused by my words, Mohammad giggled.

'You couldn't have shown him your ID, could you?' I stupidly asked.

'Of course not, we purposely leave our IDs behind,' explained the gladiator.

'Why didn't you tell us before? Both Suad and I made sure to bring our IDs with us,' complained Mohammad.

'If you're caught with your West Bank ID and no work permit the soldiers beat you up, tear up or confiscate your ID and throw you in prison immediately. But if you have no ID you can always claim that you are an Arab from Israel who has forgotten his ID at home.'

'You also get beaten up, but at least your ID isn't torn into pieces,' Mohammad observed.

So much for looking Israeli, I thought to myself. It takes much more than a pair of sunglasses to escape one's looks, one's class and one's nationality. But I also thanked God that some 10–15 percent of Palestinians stayed behind in 1948 so as to give us a cover sixty years later.

'What next?' I was feeling impatient.

'We've got to try once more,' said Saed.

'And what if the driver asks again?' I tried to hide my concern.

'*Basita*, simple, we get off and try a third time, a fourth time, a fifth time, as long as it takes.'

Having noticed that Mohammad and I were much more concerned about not being allowed on the bus than the three musketeers, Saed looked at Mohammad and said, 'Don't worry, *you* and *her* get on the next bus and we will stay behind.'

'What do you mean, *you* and *her*?' asked Mohammad, surprised, while I kept quiet.

'You look like a *khawaja* (a well-dressed signore) and you're in good company. So for sure you'll make it there; just get on that bus and tell the driver you want to get off at the Segula Station in Petah Tikva.'

'Man, are you crazy? What Segula Station? You seem to have forgotten why we're with you in the first place.' I could see that Mohammad was panicking.

'Yes indeed, why *are* you with us? I never really understood,' Saed said, half joking.

'Stop it you two, we'll all make it together to Petah Tikva, just be patient. Anyway, the day is over. What's the hurry? Remember the other day, we were seventeen workers and we all got on the Ariel bus. Just relax,' said Muneer in his over-confident comradely voice. He paused for a while and then continued, 'Why don't you and Suad go on the bus first then we follow suit? This will probably work.'

Before I had a chance to grasp our new strategy and reflect on it, or even enhance our chances by looking a bit feminine by taking off my cap and fluffing my long pressed-down hair, Ariel bus number 185 pulled in. I avoided looking into the passengers' eyes, and following Comrade Muneer's instructions I went first this time, Mohammad went second, then I lost count.

'Five tickets please,' I said in an attempt at an English accent (which probably sounded more Arabic than anything else) and a sweet pseudo smile as I handed him the fifty shekels. I could sense that the driver was a bit hesitant, probably detecting my nervous smile. Before he handed me the five tickets, he looked at me and then at the four passengers just behind me, but I grabbed the tickets and proceeded. For the first time, the *shabab* young men were all dragging behind me. The stares were doubled and shifted in the direction of the bus aisle now.

A little victory . . . at last.

I searched for two empty seats next to one another, but there were hardly any seats left. I sat next to a soldier who was asleep (or pretending to be asleep) while Mohammad settled next to an old man. Murad sat next to a young woman soldier who was looking out of the window away from him. Saed and Muneer found no seats and so stood next to the middle door.

Looking sideways, I examined the rifle right next to my leg. I felt self-conscious and nervous. For a while I kept quiet but once I had gotten used to the idea that all was fine, I wanted to talk to Mohammad, who sat two rows in front of me, on the opposite side. But speaking in Arabic, I thought, would make the passengers around me equally nervous. I was so apprehensive that I contemplated speaking to Mohammad in English, a language he didn't understand, or even in Italian, a language I hadn't mastered yet.

Just as I was resigned to the fact that it would be best if I kept quiet, I heard Murad calling my name and his brother Mohammad's as loudly as he could. From his seat, he stretched and twisted his thin neck back, looking in our direction and then out of the window,

'Look, look, look . . . look out there . . . that's where my brother Maher slept for a whole year.'

Murad stretched his arm at full length, almost touching the protruding nose of the woman soldier sitting right next to him. She pulled her head back. I looked out at where Murad was still pointing. I saw no building, just empty land. I was encouraged to ask him in Arabic 'Where?'

'There was a huge orange grove over there. The Israeli army pulled up hundreds of orange trees so that no Arab workers could spend the night there . . .'

Murad looked like a comfortable tourist guide on a friendly bus in a familiar site. The eyes of many tourists seemed to follow what he was saying.

'Maher's *'arisheh* canopy was wonderful. He constructed it in the middle of the *bayyarah* wooden tree house on top of the biggest orange tree. It had two floors: one down where he received guests and another, his bedroom, up the ladder. *Ya salam,* how wonderful it was . . . really splendid. He was like a king, before the army threw him and dozens of other Arab workers out. One day they returned home from work and the orange trees had been uprooted and a whole grove bulldozed upside down.'

Murad's vivid and animated description made me recall the way my dad used to describe orange groves around his hometown of Jaffa before 1948. Who knows, they could very well have been the same orange groves. Unlike Murad, who seemed to be familiar with the place, I had absolutely no clue where I was.

I was admiring how confident, at ease and at home Murad looked, and how uncomfortable and self-conscious some of the passengers close to him were.

Especially me.

Me, who had always considered myself a sea girl from the coastal town of Jaffa, which probably was only a stone's throw from the orange groves Murad was pointing to. I felt totally

129

alienated from the unrecognisable places and landscape, from the estrangement of the language, from the awkwardness of being on a bus with the Israeli passengers, from the cruelty of the soldiers, from the unfairness of history, from the lack of logic, and from the unbearable 'reality'. While Murad, supposedly the mountain boy from the little village of Mazare' in-Nobani in the central highlands, the heart of the peasantry, was clearly feeling totally at home.

What was home after all? Wasn't this home for Murad and friends? Wasn't it home for those who had been coming to this place for seven out of the twenty-one years that was Murad's age? Coming here for one-third of his life, and all his adult life, which had started at the age of thirteen, as there was hardly a childhood for young Palestinians like Murad and his friends.

Murad must've felt a strong sense of entitlement to this land. He gave this place his hard work, his cheap labour, his energy and his strong muscles. He understood that, in spite of it all, there was someone here who still needed him. Whenever he managed to get to the slave market in Petah Tikva, sooner or later someone would pick him up and give him work and the hundred and fifty shekels a day, and in return he would give them his life. They needed him as much as he needed them, and that he understood.

Murad simply understood the complexity of the situation; unfairly and unbearably real.

It occurred to me that this was perhaps why the second Israeli bus driver turned a blind eye to Murad and his fellow workers. If this bus driver had been on this line for the last seven years, Murad and friends would've been the most regular passengers and hence the most familiar faces. So much for my English accent and fake smile. I began to feel relaxed about it all. After all, as the Arabic saying goes: the land belongs to the one who ploughs it, *Al-ard li ili bizraha*.

Now I understood why Murad was so fearless all along. I recalled what he told me as he was tilling the soil in my Ramallah garden, the day I decided to accompany him: 'The Israeli soldiers, they run after me. Sometimes I manage to hide or run away from them, other times they arrest me; they beat me up and throw me back behind the checkpoint,' said Murad as he sipped his tea.

'"If we see you or catch you one more time, you'll never see the light of day again," one soldier told me. I kept quiet. "Do you hear us?" Followed by a slap on my head. "Yes," I told them. "Go away now." I pretended to be going *sharqa*, east (towards the West Bank), I waited for them to disappear and then I turned my back and went *gharba*, west (towards Israel). Believe me, I got back to Petah Tikva on foot before they reached it in their jeep.' Murad fell quiet, then continued, 'Once a soldier told me, "If you just tell me how you manage to come back so quickly, I swear to God I won't arrest you." Once he took me in his jeep, threw me as far as Jenin and told me, "Okay, let's race and see who gets to Petah Tikva first."'

'And?' I asked.

Murad laughed.

'Murad, you'll win in the end,' I told him as I picked up the teacups, turned and left him alone.

Having understood and acquired Murad's attitude, all of a sudden I was less self-conscious about speaking my own language. His Arabic words, mine too, sounded normal in the midst of a sea of Hebrew. If the majority of the passengers had decided to wipe out the Arabs and their language from *their* history and from *their* memory, I was sure that the land, at which Murad was pointing, still remembered that Arabic had been its language not so long ago.

I looked out of the window. The silence of this land enchanted me; how much this land knew and how little it said, and how little *they* pretended to know and how much they uttered. The power of silence and the eternal memory of this land somehow reassured me.

'Suad, Mohammad, *yalla,* let's get off here.'

Only then did I realise that for me, and many others, Israel was virtual. For Murad, Israel was 'home'. Israel was a reality; a harsh reality.

15.

Lost Chapter

Sunday May 13, 2007 [2:35 PM]
Petah Tikva

Off the bus, I diligently followed Murad and the rest. Muneer said goodbye and simply walked away. All seemed normal and fine. Petah Tikva looked like any other middle-sized town I knew. Not exactly pretty, but so what? Loads of cars, buses and trucks drove along a four-lane road, two in each direction. An all-green bus with a big white 'X' on its side drew my attention. As did the few small Ford buses, whose retirement homes and graveyards (with passengers or without) rested in the West Bank.

At an intersection of two wide roads, some pedestrians patiently waited for the white walk sign, while others went ahead and crossed on red, causing a few honks and beeps. Some gave the impression of being in a rush, probably for a high-tech industry appointment,* while others seemed more relaxed, not only about time, but also about life generally. A few strolled aimlessly along the town's wide pavements; others accompanied their little ones back from school. A young blonde mother quietly pushed the stroller of her cute tiny baby, while teenage boys on skateboards, as in other places, obtrusively jumped and skidded.

* Petah Tikva industrial zones now house the Israeli headquarters for several multinational companies.

Many, mostly men, enjoyed a cold beer or a hot meal in the modest restaurants that were dotted along a section of the main road. The smell of barbequed meat made me realise how hungry I had been all this time. I looked at my watch. It was a quarter to three in the afternoon. My companions must've been equally as starved. Realising how anxious they were to get to work, I kept my hunger pangs and suffering to myself.

I don't know why, since I'd stopped asking and they'd stopped talking altogether, but we'd mostly walked on a wide brick island in the middle of the four-lane road. Only later did I come to realise that this doubled Murad and Saed's chances of being picked up by employers coming from either direction in their cars.

My hunger vibes must have hit Murad and Saed, as they suggested we first head towards Rifqa's restaurant.

'Are we to *see*, I mean, are we to meet Lily?' I asked enthusiastically. I got a few cute smiles, but not a single response. It seemed they were hungry for love.

I was ashamed of my lack of romance.

Well, I hoped that such love might come with fresh cold mint lemonade to quench my thirst, and at least a falafel sandwich. Having appropriated the whole country, it would've been silly or petty to argue over whose national sandwich falafel was. No, not under the circumstances of a cross-cultural, cross-national, cross-religious, cross-colour and, most importantly, cross-country love story: that of Lily and Murad. Or was it . . . Lily and Saed? We were soon to find out.

In spite of his rendezvous, or perhaps because of it, Murad was constantly on the phone, alternating between his peasant

Arabic accent and his, I assume, working-class Hebrew. From his many phone conversations I figured out that Murad hadn't given up for the day. He and Saed were still hunting for a job, at least for 'the remains of the day'.

We carried on walking along the same road in the direction of Rifqa's restaurant. In reality I was also as keen on meeting Rifqa. Soon I spotted the high-rise building in front of which Murad and Lily had posed for the photo in the album.

'Is this the same building?' I joyfully asked. At last I recognised something in this totally unfamiliar place. I must say that a strong sense of estrangement got hold of me the minute I set foot in 'Israel proper' or '1948 Palestine'. Not just that time, because of my exhaustion, but almost every single time I had ever crossed that no-more 'Green Line'*. It was only in Israel–Palestine that I understand what a love–hate relationship truly meant. There was no other place on this planet that I felt so out of place, so out of space, so out of time, so out of history, so out of meaning, so out of logic, so out of my skin, and so outraged as when I was in my historic 'homeland Palestine'.

But let's leave that for now. I stretched my arm over the food counter and shook hands with a plump, fake-blonde, middle-aged woman, who I presumed was Rifqa, and a tall, sort of handsome young man.

'Hello,' I greeted both in English.

'*Shalom*,' she replied.

There's one thing I've never understood: if Israelis can greet the world using the Hebrew word *Shalom*, then why

* Green Line is an expression used by the Israeli left in reference to the 1948 borders between Israel and the West Bank.

don't we Arabs go around the world saying *As-salamo 'alai-kum*? Why did I address her in English anyway? I should've greeted her in Arabic in the first place. Come on Suad, don't be petty, it was only a hello, after all.

I passed a food counter, a long refrigerated food display, and joined the last three musketeers inside the tiny restaurant. Having swiftly examined all the food on offer, and in spite of my starvation, I still prayed none of it would make it to our table. A quick glance made me decide it was an appropriate time to start a hunger strike against humanity. But I tell you, in spite of its thin plastic cushioning, I was delighted to have that big derriere of mine rest on the green iron chair.

Like locals, or family members, both Murad and Saed went and fetched a big bottle of cold Sprite and a few plastic cups and placed them on the not-so-clean brown laminated surface of our table. I snatched a few paper towels from an aluminium box placed on the edge of our formica table and wiped it twice. Wow: I gulped, gulped and gulped half of the one-and-a-half-litre bottle of chilled Sprite. As soon as my blood had turned into thick sweet molasses, I resumed my architectural analysis: the restaurant was small and shabby, and the ceiling was made out of metal sheets supported by thin red beams going every which way. From an architect's point of view, the roof looked very unsafe. The floor had cheap ceramic pink tiles patterned with broad white cracks. The same tiles were also used for the wall around the grill area.

Right behind me was an abandoned aluminium falafel stand that was used for storage, and on top of that was a big nylon bag of paper tissues bought by the kilo. Behind a working table covered with a plastic tablecloth stood the young man who was diligently helping Rifqa. His black T-shirt contrasted strongly with the light pink and yellow roses of the tablecloth. Placed on the same table was a light blue plastic container holding white plastic cutlery: knives, forks and spoons. It felt like we were in the backyard of Petah Tikva's famous plastic factory. Except for the natural light coming from a high window, the elongated and narrow room was lit by a series of alternating neon lights.

My architectural dissatisfaction came to an end with a two-minute visit from Rifqa. She placed a very long silver knife on the working table, and came around the counter to join us. She sat right next to me.

'Are you Lily's mum?' I asked her in Arabic (a small revenge, I thought). Smiling, she answered back in broken Arabic and a very heavy Israeli accent, 'No, Lily is not my daughter!' She seemed a bit surprised.

'I am Murad's mother.'

'No you're not,' she smiled.

'This is Mohammad, he is Murad's brother,' I continued.

'No he's not,' she insisted.

'We came to ask for Lily's hand.' I tell you she got a kick out of that. She laughed and laughed and laughed.

'She is not my daughter, she once worked for me.' She couldn't stop laughing; she had tears in her tiny dark brown eyes.

'Any chance of seeing her before we leave this afternoon?' I asked.

'Don't think so . . . she passes by every now and then, but I doubt very much she'll come by today.'

137

There was a moment of silence around the table. Perhaps all were a bit taken aback by my menopausal directness and lack of graciousness.

'If you were Saed's mother, you may have had a better chance of meeting her.' Laughter exploded from her as she pulled her seat back and stood up to leave. Her hysterical laughter made me miss Ramzi.

'Oh. I see what you're saying,' I responded, amused.

'What is in the heart is in the heart, *illi fil qalb fil qalb*,' replied Mohammad philosophically. Since he was the one to start the joke about 'asking for Lily's hand', Mohammad was defending his joke, his family's reputation and, above all, his brother Murad who had, meanwhile, stepped out, together with Saed, to the front terrace of the restaurant. He was still talking on the phone. There was only Mohammad and me left at the table. She ended her brief break by greeting us again in Arabic, *Ahlan wa sahlan,* and went back to serving her many customers.

For a while, Mohammad and I opted for more Sprite and a few preventive visits to the toilet just in case.

'What are you two up to?' enquired Murad, while he and Saed stood there in a sprinter's position: on your marks . . . get set . . . go . . .

'If *ma'limti*, my boss, agrees, I would *love* to go to the beach in Tel Aviv,' replied little spoiled brat Mohammad. I couldn't believe my ears.

'For God's sake, Mohammad, what beach, what Tel Aviv? I want to accompany them to the workers' market in Segula,' I replied, somewhat ashamed of my companion's frivolous desires.

'Bus 82 will take you there. But make sure to get off the bus before Tel Aviv's main bus station otherwise the security men will nail you. They'll arrest you for sure, that's no joke; no Arab worker ever makes it there.'

'Hey . . . hey . . . hey . . . wait a second you two, we're not going to the beach, and we don't intend to get arrested. We came all this way so you could get a job. Come *on* Mohammad, stop it.'

Mohammad kept quiet, which meant he hadn't totally given up on his idea. After twelve years of working together, I knew him pretty well.

'But there's nothing to see. Murad and I will hang around for an hour or so, and since it is already . . . what?' he looked at his watch, 'three-thirty, most probably we'll not be able to find work today. We'll have to come back tomorrow at five, maximum five-thirty, so as to be picked up first thing in the morning,' explained Saed.

'Okay, let's go give it a try then,' I insisted as I collected my cap and silly sunglasses.

While I took my time thanking Rifqa for her hospitality, Murad gave her twenty shekels which she accepted matter-of-factly. To my disappointment she wasn't as generous as Mazen had tried to make out the night before. As we passed through Rifqa's restaurant's busy front terrace and along the road, I understood that we were being kept backstage.

Saed was right: there was nothing striking or special about Petah Tikva's Segula workers' market. I somehow had the image in my head of a proper market, a *souq,* a square where many Arab workers sold their services and many Yahoodi employers haggled over prices. I thought it would be an elaborate version of the workers' market in East Jerusalem before that stupid highway (Route 1), which separated East Jerusalem from West Jerusalem, cut through it. I don't know why but everything the Israelis did to 'unite' the 'eternal' capital seemed to separate Arabs and Jews even more. Anyway, the workers' market or 'hang out' point was basically a strip of that same main road.

Sensing that Murad and Saed were (more than) a bit tired or nervous about still having us around, we distanced ourselves from them. Mohammad and I stood along one side of the road while Murad and Saed stood in the middle island of the road.

Considering it was past three-thirty in the afternoon, there were still a few workers around. Some stood on our side of the road, a few more sat on the metal railing on the opposite side, and more insistent or keener workers, such as Murad and Saed, stood in the middle. I sat on a low plantation edge on the sidewalk next to a worker who was about the same age as the boy-in-red.

'Did you just arrive?' I asked, assuming he'd made the same trip with us that day.

'No, I came yesterday, Saturday afternoon, and stood here all day today, but no one's picked me up so far.'

Considering how soft his muscles and bones looked, and how Israel was all about survival of the fittest, I wasn't surprised.

'Just hang around a bit more and I am sure someone will eventually pick you up.' These were the most profound words I could manage.

'Why don't you two leave?' I heard Saed yell from among the cars that zipped in both directions. With his back to us, Murad was concentrating on slower-moving cars.

'Okay, Mohammad, let's go.' I stood up and waved good-bye to Saed and Murad. I shook hands with the young boy next to me. I turned my back and walked away from it all. I didn't want to be a witness to what may happen if only *one* car pulled in and asked for only *one* worker for that afternoon. Mohammad and I went back along the same road. I had no clue if Mohammad knew his way around; I didn't know what was next, and had no desire to even ask.

A sense of emptiness took hold of me
A sense of resentment took hold of me
A sense of indignation took hold of me
A sense of worthlessness took hold of me
A sense of purposelessness took hold of me
A sense of valuelessness took hold of me
A sense of rage took hold of me
A sense of hatred took hold of me.

I wiped my tears.

'You must be tired and hungry,' said Mohammad.

I was ashamed of myself
I was ashamed of my people
I was ashamed of this world.

And I was ashamed of you, Petah Tikva, yes you, Petah Tikva, the 'Port of Hope', the 'Mother of Settlements' and the 'Birth Place of the Zionist Labour Movement'. If you were the 'Port of Hope', I wondered what the Lack of Hope would be like. If you were the 'Mother of Settlements', I didn't want to know what took place in the 'Father of Settlements', or in any other 'members of the family' settlements. If this was the 'Birth Place' of a leftist labour movement', I didn't want to imagine how Arab workers were treated by right-wing labour movements.

'Suad, let's sit in this park for a few minutes in order to figure out what next,' Mohammad hesitantly .

Cautiously I sat on the abundantly watered green lawn. I was in no mood to share with Mohammad my fears about being in a 'park' in Israel. A haunting fear took hold of me as I thought about the real story behind Israel's many 'parks', 'nature reserves' and 'forests'. Like many, at first, I was environmentally impressed, then I was humanly horrified to realise that Jewish National Fund parks contained the remains of some eighty-six destroyed Arab villages such as the village of Amuka in the Biriya Forest; Reihaniyeh in the Ramat Menashe Park; Jimzu in the Ben Shemen Forest; Saraa in the Tzora Forest; Ajur in Park Britain; Yalo, 'Emwas and Biet Nuba in Canada Park; and so on it shamefully went.

But it was Murad and his friends that kept referring to Petah Tikva as Mlabbis, the name of the Arab village which was demolished by the Israelis, and on whose lands Petah Tikva was first built and continued to expand. And here we were, Mohammad and I, sitting, innocently enjoying the lavish 'park' with many other Israelis, from all walks of life, including a few Arab workers who had obviously given up for the day.

I took a few steps away from everyone, including Mohammad, and threw myself next to a pseudo-Calder mobile sculpture. The brownish red metal forms, right above me, violated the very concept and spirit of Calder's

142

light suspended mobiles that were based on movement and balance. This badly jointed metal structure was far from being free-spirited or elegant. Anyway, why should this sculpture be more honest about its origins than the park in which it stood? If Israel had violated every other law on this planet, why should Calder's laws of balance and movement be respected? I lay on my back, my two arms stretched parallel next to my head, knees bent, cap and silly dark brown glasses shading the low rays of the sun and the tears.

I wondered if I was lying in the middle of the Mlabbis graveyard.
I wondered if my head was resting on one of the villagers' collarbones.
Or was I in someone's living room?
Or in somebody's bed?
I took a few deep breaths, shifting to more positive thinking, and let my thoughts and mind wander in the narrow alleys of the once lively tiny Arab hamlet of Mlabbis.

I took a stroll in the different *harat*, the family-based quarters. I took the liberty of entering many *ahwash*, semi-private courtyards.
Old men and old women sat on *masateb*, elevated platforms right in front of their homes, warming their frail bodies in the soft afternoon May sun.
Half-naked little children ran after one another or chased hens that ran just as fast and, when need be, flew up and took time out on piles of rubble.
Sniffing little rabbits hid from it all behind their tranquil mothers.

The sound of kids yelling and hens clucking were every now and then swollen by the honking of an aged, forgotten donkey tied to an almond tree.

I took a peek into one of the peasants' small mud-and-stone houses. The coolness of its interior pulled me in and refreshed my soul and ailing body, as did the welcoming gesture and whispers of a young mother humming while nursing her few-days-old baby, his full-moon face resembling his gracious-looking mother.

I patted the little cat next to them, which closed its sleepy eyes and purred. I imbibed from a small ceramic water pitcher placed in one of the many little alcoves in the whitewashed walls, some of which had pots and pans, while others had oil lamps. I noted, admired and couldn't resist touching the intricate decorations of the *nileh*, the pitcher: the blue crescents and stars and brown henna palm trees.

I opened the tops of mud-baked storage bins that were filled with lentils, dried figs and raisins. I never ceased to take pride in my gender's artistic talents and never-ending chores. I admired the *qus*, the neatly stacked mattresses placed in big alcoves. I contemplated spreading out in the vast empty space next to the unlit *wijaq* fireplace. I knew better: if I lay down on one of those mattresses my deep and endless sleep would end the story right there and then. And that I didn't want, for in spite of my fatigue, their *whole* story must be told. I nodded goodbye, and for good luck, with my right foot, I stepped over the stone threshold of the house.

I soon followed that familiar mouth-watering smell, an odour similar to Um Maher's *taboun* oven. I couldn't tell whether it was the smell of the roast chicken or the heat

144

emanating from that oven that drew me closer to some of the Mlabbis women who had gathered to bake bread and grill a few chickens. I enjoyed the village gossip but could hardly follow who had married who, who was the lucky woman who gave birth to a baby boy, and who was the woman who cried day and night, having given birth to yet *another* baby girl named Nihayyeh ('the end').

In the centre of the village I passed a one-room boys' school, a *kuttab*, the yells and shrieks giving me the impression that there were far more boys than girls in this village. They were repeating and reciting after their blind teacher. Some had brought him a few eggs, while others had brought him some freshly made yogurt. This was his 'fee in kind' in appreciation for his endless efforts to teach them how to read the Quran and hence learn the Arabic language and its impossible grammar. I looked everywhere for a girls' school but failed to find one.

In my meanderings, I passed little girls acrobatically carrying water jars on their heads. I followed their well-balanced little steps until I reached the village's *'ein,* its spring. I bent down, twisted my protruding lips and sipped and sipped its crystal pure icy water until I was clean and Sprite-sugar-free.

From a distance I could hear the ringing bells of a herd. I stood under a huge carob tree and watched the skinny black goats give a young shepherd boy a hard time. As the sheep flocked obediently into a circular pen, goats ran everywhere; some jumped onto steep rocks, others munched on low fig tree branches, and a few stretched their bodies along tree trunks. I love that goatish rebellious and insubordinate spirit.

In the midst of the village's rolling hills, mostly in its gilded wheat fields, I saw many men and women still working.

Ah . . . of course, I remembered, May was the month of harvest in the busy agricultural cycle. The wheat harvest meant the end of spring, the fig and grape harvest meant the end of summer, the olive harvest meant the end of autumn. And the forty days' wet and cold *marba'nieh* meant: get some rest, get used to the cold and then get ready for pruning the early spring vegetable and cereal plantations.

I sat at one end of a *baidar*, a huge natural flat millstone, and joyfully watched the two mules going in circles, dragging behind them a long wooden milling board, *midras*, on which two relatively small-sized men sat as weights. In spite of my utter fatigue, I joined the women in tossing the threshed wheat up into the air so as to separate the heavy grains from the hay. I also gave a hand to older women who bundled heaps of wheat and carried them home just before sunset.

I trailed behind older women who were mounted on donkeys totally covered with bundles of hay. I listened to their complaints, and finally tried to get away from an incessant moaning . . . I took a shortcut through the village's main *saha* plaza. The whys and wows aroused my curiosity. I stood close by the men's *madafeh* or guesthouse and eavesdropped. Elderly men from Mlabbis, and from other neighbouring Arab villages, had gathered to urgently discuss what seemed to be a heatedly disputed 'land deal'. They argued about the 'morality' and the 'legality' of someone selling thirty-four *dunum*s (thirty-four-thousand square metres) to five religious Jews from Jerusalem. Some argued that it was an act of treason, while others believed it was an act of friendly coexistence: a new, modern and well-organised Jewish agricultural settlement right next to an organic indigenous Arab village.

But no one seemed to be aware of what was awaiting them in the not so distant future.

A land with no people for a people with no land.

But whatever the verdict was that day, and whatever the inhabitants thought or didn't think, at the end of the day, Petah Tikva was built and expanded on beyond the disputed or non-disputed lands of Mlabbis. And as bad times went by, the confiscation of Arab lands became a common, everyday practice.

It was on a sunny May day like today that the Israeli forces attacked the village of Mlabbis. In terror they had all run away, leaving behind their hens and chickens, their goats and donkeys, their horses and mules, dogs and cats, including one contentedly purring cat.

It was on that same sunny day in May that a dog barked and barked, barked and barked, until someone came running back in order to fetch Ali: that old man who had been left behind in the midst of the havoc. In spite of the old man's many and never-ending Mlabbis stories and legends, which started with Noah's ark and never ended, his memory froze with that one story: the day they had all run away and left him behind.

'But here you are with all of us, Grandpa, in the refugee camp of eternity,' said grandchild Ali giggling.

'What do you know, little Ali? They all ran away and left me behind with the village livestock and animals,' insisted Grandpa Ali. Little Ali looked at me and tried hard to explain. But Ali's grandfather was no different; a whole nation's memory had frozen right there and then, and a whole world was trying hard to wipe out his grandfather's memory. But memories are spirit-like: they have the ability to reincarnate.

It was on a sunny May day like today, a year later, that some tried to come back to harvest their fields when the inhabitants of the new town nearby fired on them and they, once more, ran away.

It was on a sunny May day like today that the neighbours' bulldozers arrived in order to level to the ground the houses, schools, guesthouses, stone walls, trees and bread oven. There were so many organic remains that a park was eventually declared.

It was on Israel's Independence May Day, like today, some sixty years later, that many of the inhabitants of the Newly Born State complained that on a sunny and fresh May day like today some could still feel the ghosts and the spirits of the many destroyed Arab villages.

It was on a sunny May day like today that Murad and his friends stood on parts of *their* Mlabbis land and waited for a friendly neighbour in a passing car to give them something small in return.

16.

194. Lost Right of Return*

My multiple May daydreams came to an end as I listened to Mohammad talking on the phone. It seemed that both Murad and Saed had already succeeded in getting some work. From the scraps of the phone conversation, I figured out that it was the same friendly and sympathetic woman that often gave him and Saed some work in her big and lavish garden.

'She'll pay them five hundred shekels,' Mohammad bragged, as if it was his own doing. I wanted to ask if it was five hundred each, but thought I was getting greedy. I also wanted to ask about the weak-muscled boy but decided to stop and look at the bright side of life. With such great news, I opened my eyes, jumped up from the ground and yelled as I dusted my backside, 'All right, *mission accomplished*, let's go to Tel Aviv,' a big smile on my face.

'You don't really mean it, Suad, do you?' It seemed that my tears had deterred Mohammad from talking to me. Had it not been for my own initiative, we would have remained in the Mlabbis graveyard for the rest of our lives.

* Right of Return refers to the 1948 UN Security Council Resolution no. 194, which gives the Palestinian refugees the right to go back to their homes and/or compensation for their properties in what had become the state of Israel.

'Of course I mean it. Let's go celebrate in Tel Aviv.'
'Celebrate!'

'Come on, Mohammad, let's go: you go to the Zionist capital Tel Aviv, and I go to my Arab hometown Jaffa.'

'It's a deal, let's go.' Action was Murad-like, faster than words. Mohammad was already on the move. With a sudden change of mood, I wanted to fulfill Mohammad's desire to have a swim on one of Tel Aviv's sandy beaches, and my desire to have a yummy dinner in one of Jaffa's splendid fish restaurants, not far from what was once my father's home in *Al-Manshiyyeh,* an Arab neighbourhood between Tel Aviv and Jaffa.

Being so far our fourth or fifth bus ride of the day, it was no sweat. As instructed by Murad, Mohammad and I got on bus 83 taking us from Petah Tikva all the way to the very heart of Tel Aviv. There was no need, and no energy, to speak to one another in Arabic; nor, for that matter, in any other language. We simply collapsed next to one another, me on a window seat and he on an aisle. Mohammad reclined his seat as far back as possible, shut his eyes and, in no time, he and I had surrendered to the rhythmic hum of his soft snores.

I rested my heavy head on the glass and looked out of the window. I was still annoyed by my unfamiliarity with a place only a few kilometres away from Jaffa. Everything around me looked so alien, and so unattractive (and believe me, that was not a political stand). The silver poles of the many traffic lights, the exaggerated size of the electrical metal trusses and the childish lollipop colours painted on the many electrical boxes (one electric box was painted bright blue with huge rose balloons or distorted pomegranates), all contributed to the shabbiness of the place. Billboards hung everywhere. There were freestanding billboards on every main road intersection, on every bus that passed by and on every cement building along that main road. The brown façade of a three-storey building was *totally* covered by three huge billboards, one red and white, one bright purple and one with the colours of the Israeli flag, white and blue. Since the writing was only in Hebrew they all lost me as a potential customer.

Soon the bus drove us from Petah Tikvah's industrial zone to more residential-looking areas. The 1950s low-cost four-storey buildings (referred to in Hebrew as *shikunut*) that lined the sides of the main road leading to Tel Aviv looked truly dreadful and harsh. The balconies, typical of Mediterranean apartment buildings, were somehow missing. The iron safety bars installed on their small windows made them look more like prisons. They were so poor and humble compared to the huge stone mansions built in some of the Israeli settlements on the West Bank. No wonder that the majority of Israelis felt jealous of the settlers' many privileges. The majority of Israelis hated the settlers to the point where they insisted that the settlers must remain with us, on the West Bank.

What annoyed me most was the lack of character and lack of spirit; the place was neither here nor there. It did not have the sophistication of the new and modern cities or the charm of the old and traditional place that it had once been. It had that nondescript emptiness of American suburbia. It was neither European nor Arab-looking. I guess it simply looked what it was: Israeli. How could historic Palestine have become so alien so quickly to its original Arab inhabitants? I guess what disturbed me most was the fact that I couldn't spot one single Arab house in memory of the three-quarters-of-a-million

Palestinians that had been driven out of their homeland, my family being one of them, sixty years earlier.

Perhaps the only redeeming factor was the lavish dark green of its Mediterranean plantations: flowering purple jacarandas, blooming bell-like orange begonias, white jasmines, red hibiscus, blue wisterias, Cypress trees, pines and eucalyptus trees. I searched for indigenous trees, trees favoured by Palestinians, and which I now had in my Ramallah garden – fig trees, pomegranate, mulberry, walnut, almond and plum – but I found none. What added to my strong sense of estrangement was the absence of a single orange tree, although we must have been in the close vicinity of the famous Jaffa oranges.

Soon we arrived at a modern urban setting. The high-rise aluminium and glass buildings made me think that we were approaching or already in Tel Aviv. I was looking to my right in an attempt to spot the sea so I could say, 'Wake up, Mohammad, desire fulfilled.' But before I managed to orientate myself and figure out where we were, the bus took a sharp right and went into what looked liked the . . . No, it couldn't be . . . it shouldn't be . . . it was . . . yes, the Central Bus Station.

Oh God, this was the one place that Murad made sure to warn us not to venture into. His words echoed in my spinning head: *No Arab makes it there, and if he does, he'll be arrested for sure.*

Having complete confidence in Murad and his sharp sense of danger, I was truly worried. In no time the bus stopped, and in less time a dark-looking security man got on the bus. I didn't have time to judge if it was better to wake Mohammad up or leave him asleep. The security man was staring in every passenger's face. Not spotting Arab-looking faces, he moved swiftly and efficiently until he reached our row. I looked away from him and prayed he didn't have the necessary training or skills to spot a middle-aged, sexless Arab woman or a sleeping young Arab or a sleeping terrorist. From the corner of my eye I saw him glance at Mohammad; he stooped for a fraction of a second but soon moved on. Wow. What a relief. Once the security man had descended from the bus I gently pushed Mohammad, once, twice, three times before he woke up.

'Where are we?' he asked as he rubbed his sleepy red eyes.

'In the place where we are *not* supposed to be.'

'Really! Are we in the Central Bus Station?' He jumped from his seat.

'Sit down, Mohammad, the security man has already checked the bus and decided you were a sleeping beauty,' I whispered.

Mohammad and I got off that bus knowing that we'd both missed out on our desires. We realised it would be safest if we gave them up, for the time being, and took the bus from Tel Aviv to Jerusalem. Another security check was waiting for us at the entrance of the station, and once more we successfully passed the non-Arab-looking test. At the booth, I bought two tickets to Jerusalem and hurriedly went and sat on the half-empty bus taking us to West Jerusalem.

Feeling a bit relieved that we had made it out of Tel Aviv Station, Mohammad enquired again, 'Really, Suad, what happened?'

'Well, you fell asleep and I somehow lost my way to the sea: so much for the Right of Return to our home in Jaffa; even if one day Israel accepts the refugees' right of return, we would probably lose our way back home.'

Before I knew it, Mohammad had shut his heavy red eyes and resumed his swimming in the sea of dreams. I sank into a window seat and tirelessly watched the world go backwards. The half-empty bus zoomed out of Tel Aviv's grid street pattern into the bustling Tel Aviv-Jerusalem highway. It somehow felt simple and easy. During our early months of dating, whenever Salim and I ran away from Ramallah, venturing on a rendezvous in our two families' hometown of Jaffa, consciously or subconsciously we would get lost in a maze of narrow and crooked alleys. It often took some time before we'd figure out how to make it to this very same highway. Not wanting to spend the night in Jaffa, certainly not in Tel Aviv, my anxiety would mount and so would Salim's hopes.

'Why not spend the night here?' Salim would naughtily propose, and I would playfully reply, 'It is against the law . . . I mean the Israeli law . . . I mean it is illegal to spend the night in Israel without a permit, even in Jaffa.' My law-abiding and beating-around-the-bush comments would be followed by laughs, giggles and a toss of my head onto his shoulders. The car would swirl.

'Don't give me that . . . you've been "illegal" since your visitor's permit expired six or seven months ago.'

Unlike the Petah Tikva-Tel Aviv road, I was a bit familiar with this highway, even though Salim and I hadn't sneaked into Israel, or Jaffa, for almost a decade now (we hadn't been dating either). Driving on this highway brought back all sorts of joyful and melancholic images and memories. Soon the bus was driving through relatively familiar grounds: high-rise buildings, a few factories, depot areas, big farms whose roofs

154

had slanting red tiles and beautiful vast green and reddish brown open fields. The three-language road signs in Hebrew, English and the misspelled Arabic indicated 'Ben-Gurion Airport'. Not only had they changed its Arabic name, Al-Lid or Lod Airport (1948–1973) and misspelled it, but they had also made sure to write it in the most primitive handwriting. Having a profound love of Arabic calligraphy, that terrible third-class handwriting really got to me.

Regardless of its disputed name and the shameful history of Lod and Ben-Gurion, I somehow missed that airport. Yes, I missed that bloody airport. In spite of all the hardships and interrogations (and claims of dancing in London) that I had, coming in and out of it, I did miss it. I wondered if anyone, other than us Palestinians, would miss an airport. Not a lover, but an airport!

Just before he went into a long-lasting coma, Sharon issued a *firman*, a decree that no Palestinian from the West Bank or the Gaza Strip was allowed to use this airport. While most of the world had forgotten about Sharon, only us, and his family, of course, were praying that he would eventually come out of his coma to reverse this and many other insane orders. This airport was only half an hour away from my home in Ramallah, while Amman Airport, which we were forced to use now, took a day or two to reach.

'How can you do that and rest in a coma?' I found myself reprimanding Sharon.

Soon the road signs indicated the once major twin Arab towns of Al-Lid and Al-Ramleh; the signs read: 'Lod' and 'Ramla'. I couldn't be bothered again by the terrible hand-writing, but I was disturbed by the dismissive hand wave. 'Waving his hand in a gesture which said, Drive them out! . . .

Psychologically, this was one of the most difficult actions we undertook,' wrote Yitzhak Rabin in his book *Soldiers of Peace*. That hand wave of the first Israeli Prime Minister, David Ben-Gurion, resulted in the displacement of forty thousand Arabs, the inhabitants of this twin town. My heart beamed and my mood lightened as I saw a sign pointing east towards my hometown of Ramallah. Never mind the Jewish settlement of Moda'ein then Ramallah. Wasn't it amazing how we needed simple things such as a road sign to assure us that we truly existed on this land?

Once the bus started ascending the steep hills in the Latrun area, in the direction of Jerusalem, my mind began to recall the hidden stories behind the many forests, parks and nature reserves that stretched along the Tel Aviv-Jerusalem highway.

I followed the barely remaining traces of a buried but not forgotten landscape.

I saw a thick forest of fir and cypress trees planted on the remains of the Arab village 'Aqqur.

I watched the many fenced-in areas surmounting gentle hills of olive groves.

I traced the *sabber* cactus hedges (*saber* in Arabic means 'patience') that often grew in memory of the hundreds of destroyed villages.

When we passed the village of 'Allar, I saw the remains of stone walls with arched openings.

My eyes followed untended fruit trees which stood close to the two deserted small stone houses of Beit Mahsier. They stood shyly behind the new constructions of the Israeli town Beit Me'ir.

I saw beautiful pine trees around the crumbled houses and rubble of Deir al-Hawa.

I followed the beautiful houses of the deserted village of Lifta all the way down the splendid valleys that surrounded it.

I saw neglected scatterings of stone and rubble around deserted mosques and churches.

I took a deep breath when we got to the splendid village of 'Ein Karem, which was one of the few villages to survive its depopulation.

I saw the remains of a fallen fortress on top of the hill at Beit I'tab.

And finally, I purposely skipped the terrible thoughts and images of Deir Yasin, where an Israeli hospital for the mentally ill stands today.

My impossible mission to trace and reconstruct a lost world, a lost society, and perhaps a lost hope, meant I barely noticed the series of three taxi journeys that took Mohammad and I from the Central Bus Station in West Jerusalem to the American Colony Hotel in Arab East Jerusalem, and from there to Qalandia checkpoint and finally to Ramallah. I opened the front door to our home and yelled, 'Nura . . . I'm back . . .'

It took a split second for little Nura to appear, her excitement, the exaggerated wagging of her tail, the circular dance and the welcoming cries made me feel like I had been gone forever. I looked at my watch: it was ten past six in the evening.

I stepped into our bedroom
And stood in front of the long mirror: I twisted my body left . . . right . . . and centre.
I seemed sexless.

I could no longer feel the innocence of the little girl in me or the playfulness of the Big Boys.
I took off my worker's clothing.

I leaned forward
And gazed lengthily at my fatigued face.
In the dark blue lines under my sad eyes I could see Murad's sunburnt face,
I could see Abu Yousef's,
Saed's and Muneer's,
And of course that of silly Ramzi.

I slipped into the softness of the fresh cotton sheets
And closed my eyes.
I wept into my pillows.
God, all they want is work.

Nura licked the tears from my cheeks.
I smiled.

'Cool it Nunu: I couldn't have stayed with them for more than eighteen hours.'

ACKNOWLEDGEMENTS

One thing that never ceases to amaze or baffle me is how much energy, thought, emotions and time go into the creation of any meaningful work: it being a building, a song, an art work, a poem or, in this case, a book. Having written *Nothing to Lose But Your Life: An 18-hour journey with Murad* 'all by myself', I want to simply list the people and places that have been absolutely instrumental in the making of this book.

First and foremost, I thank Alberto Rollo, from Feltrinelli in Milano again and again for playing the role of an extremely 'delicate and fine writer's surgeon'. Thank you dear Alberto, for your reassuring and encouraging words, 'But Suad, you are a writer,' that often arrived at critical moments. I am most indebted to Giovanna Silvia for her valuable suggestions, her constructive and positive feedback on the Italian version, and mostly for her super sensitivity. Maria Nadotti is a friend, a faithful companion, an excellent reader and translator and, most importantly, a promoter. Thank you, Maria, for your total commitment and unconditional love and support.

I am indebted to my English editor, Suzy Joinson, who worked hard not only to transform my Arabic-sounding English into proper English but was also extremely sensitive to my voice and writing style. Thank you, Suzy, for putting up with my 'writer's fear' of cutting or changing the text. Special thanks also go to Andy Smart from Bloomsbury Qatar Foundation Publishing. I am most thankful to Ahdaf Soueif for her help and support in getting *Nothing to Lose But Your Life* published in English, and also for all she does and stands for, especially the Palestine Literature Festival (Palfest).

Very special thanks go to my friend, Penny Johnson (Baby Johnson), whose judgments I totally trust: Penny read, commented and, as always, was extremely insightful.

My husband, Salim Tamari (since the book was neither about him nor about his mum this time), was the first to read and to 'love' *Nothing to Lose But Your Life*. Coming from a critical husband like mine, his remarks and suggestions were extremely valuable.

I thank Vera Nofal and my niece, Diala Khasawneh, for being such faithful readers of all drafts of this and all my previous books. Marisa Savoia's tentative ears have always been extremely supportive: thank you, Marisa, for your continuous moral support of me and my writings. Our shared Terrazzo Paradiso in the Isola di Procida never ceases to be a magical place and a real inspiration for the writing of this book, which started there then travelled on to Ramallah, Berkeley and Boston.

Thanks also to Murad's family whose 'cushioned love' gave me the needed courage and strength to make this trip.

My gratitude goes to Mohammad, Murad's brother, for his fun and faithful companionship, not only on this difficult eighteen-hour trip, but also for the last fifteen years and hopefully for many years to come.

No words can express my gratitude to Murad and his friends. All I can say is, Murad . . . thank you for a trip that has completely changed my life and my attitude, and surfaced my anger about an 'unfair' world that you are fated to face, I am afraid, all alone. And for that, I apologise.

AUTHOR'S NOTE

The Day I finished writing *Nothing to Lose But Your Life: An 18-hour journey with Murad,* I made myself a cup of coffee, sat on the terrace, in the sun, picked up *Al-Ayyam* newspaper and read:

While Chasing Workers With No Permits:
Palestinian worker shot dead by Israeli police in Nazareth

Yesterday in Nazareth, Israeli police shot dead a Palestinian worker from the village of Muthalath al-Shuhada west of Jenin.

Palestinian sources reported they were informed by the Israelis that the Israeli police had fired at worker Majdi Mustafa Nazzal, 25 years old, in a mountainous area close to Nazareth, as they chased a group of Palestinian workers who had crossed the Green Line without the necessary permits.

The sources confirmed that Nazzal was killed instantly. His corpse was taken to an Israeli hospital.

The Nazzal family reported that he had left his home around ten in the morning to seek work in Nazareth. The family reported that their son had tried many times to get a work permit from the Israeli authorities to allow him to work inside [Israel], but all his attempts had failed. He had been forced to cross the Green Line in search of work without a permit and hence risk his life in order to make a living.

161

The Nazzal family said that Israel is fully responsible for the premeditated killing of their son. At the same time it pleaded to the Palestinian National Authority and human rights organisations to intervene and find out the details and circumstances that resulted in the crime of their son's killing. The family said that the Israeli authorities continue to retain the body of their son.

Al-Ayyam newspaper
November 15, 2008
(translated by the author)